Whispers from My Mother

Whispers from My Mother

Whispers from My Mother

Books by Samuel K. Anderson

1. God's Audacity: The Logic of God's Existence.
2. Whispers from My Mother.
3. Humans Audacity: The Leadership in Everyone.
4. The Kind Prince and Princess (Children's Book edition).
5. Ascend to Your Higher Self.
6. Energetic Vibrating Frequency.
7. NINALEM: The Dawn of a New Era.
8. Biblical Psychosis and Psychosomatics.
9. Dear Afrikans, Can You Hear Me From 500 Years Ago or 500 Years From Today!!!
10. 111 Laws and Proverbs I Wish I Knew Earlier in Life.

Whispers from My Mother

Whispers from My Mother

By
Samuel K. Anderson

Royal Publication

New Jersey, U.S.A

Whispers from My Mother

Copyright © 2019 Samuel K. Anderson.

All rights reserved. No part of this book may be reproduced or used in any manner without written permission of the copyright owner except for the use of quotations in a book review.

1ˢᵗ Edition September 2019

ISBN-10: 1-7340066-6-8

ISBN-13: 978-1-7340066-6-7 (Trade Hardback)

ISBN-10: 1-7340066-8-4

ISBN-13: 978-1-7340066-8-1 (Trade Paperback)

Royal Publication
royalpublication@aol.com
roralpublication.net

Whispers from My Mother

This book is fervently dedicated to my children: Serenity, Samuel II and Samuel III a.k.a Nana Datu

Whispers from My Mother

Table of Content

1. Into Existence
2. The Arrival
3. The Therapy
4. This is a Reality Check
5. The Seed of Discord
6. Revolve to Involve to Evolve
7. The Fine Polished One
8. I am Stupendous
9. Ponder
10. Life's Basic Units
11. The Power in Failure
12. The "Going Through"
13. I Am Being
14. External Value
15. The Strip
16. Chances vs Doubt
17. Take Caution
18. The Interrupters
19. Materialistic and Deceptive World
20. Be Extraordinary
21. Conversation between Mother & Son
22. Gift of Loyalty
23. Love Never Stops
24. Deeply Rooted
25. Say this Repetitively to Yourself
26. Diversions
27. Upside Down
28. It's a Beautiful Day
29. Be Strong
30. On Common Sense, Knowledge & Wisdom
31. Aspirations
32. The Lesson
33. Intellectual Swag
34. Sunken Place Miracle
35. The Desire
36. Introspective Affirmation
37. Common Sense Deciphering
38. The Waiting Phase
39. The Misconception
40. Conscious Reminiscing
41. The Gist
42. Your Decision, Your Choice
43. The Face Off
44. Think Through It
45. The Extraordinary
46. We Are Water
47. The Solution
48. Keep Growing
49. Greatness
50. The Truth
51. Simplistic Meaning
52. "Exit In" - "Exit Out"
53. Everything Changed
54. Today
55. Stability vs Quick Rising
56. Phases
57. I Am a god
58. Knowledge is Freedom
59. Don't Clog Your Energy
60. Confidence
61. Reflections
62. The Truth is Timeless
63. Success is Birthed
64. S. O. A. P.
65. Thankful & Blessed
66. Edification
67. Inspiration
68. Value
69. Beware
70. Mindset
71. The Power of Listening
72. May I Never Forget
73. Root
74. Conscious Awakening

Whispers from My Mother

75. Treasure
76. Trading Places
77. Life Unknown
78. Bigger, Better, Greater
79. Snap Out
80. Aha!!
81. It could Burn
82. Good Energy
83. Perspective
84. Resist Fear
85. The Highs, The Lows, The In-Betweens
86. Welcome It All
87. Unexpectedly Expected
88. You Fall to Rise
89. Conscious Energy
90. Choose to Challenge Yourself
91. The Art of Giving Up
92. The Key to Unlock
93. Fossilization by Petrification
94. Moments of Vulnerabilities
95. Illusion of Time
96. The Love Factor
97. Messengers
98. It's All About Service
99. Free

100. Psychological Freedom
101. Versatility Mindset
102. Comprennent
103. Intent of Manifestation
104. Special Self
105. Ability
106. You
107. Infinity
108. Let them flow
109. Light
110. Aeration of Your Life
111. Spiritually Awakening
112. Truce of no Repetition
113. Self-Talk
114. The Challenge
115. O. R. A. N. G. E.
116. You Have the Power
117. Over stand
118. Get It Going
119. You Are the Judge
120. Got It
121. Self-Check
122. Read it Again
123. The Reason
124. Growth
125. Genius
126. What Do You See?

127. See Me
128. Who am I
129. Addicted to Success
130. Regardless
131. Sunset
132. Joyfully
133. In It
134. Oblivion
135. Grounded
136. Characterize
137. Confide
138. Codes
139. Pause to Ponder
140. Constantly Creating - pg. 280
141. "Euphoria"
142. Aspire to Inspire
143. Ignorance
144. Exude
145. Conscious Beauty
146. Pondering
147. Infinite Love
148. Scars
149. Instead
150. Work It
151. Youthful Days
152. Distractions
153. Trust Me

Whispers from My Mother

154. It's Yours
155. Learn through Grace
156. Time to Progress - pg. 312
157. Breaks
158. "The Secret Code"
159. Precious Gift
160. Precision
161. Don't Hide
162. Seize the Moments
163. True Image
164. Sense of Smell
165. Risk
166. Plan the Plan
167. Common Denominator
168. Strategic
169. Gifted
170. The "you" within You
171. Creative
172. Insecurities
173. Get It Done
174. Never Again
175. Word
176. Clearheaded
177. Choose Peace
178. Clarity in Confusion
179. The Beauty in Humility
180. You Ready?

181. Greater and Lesser selves
182. Inward Outward
183. Unknown Known
184. Profound
185. Dare
186. Bold Faith
187. Different
188. Audacity Decoded
189. Good
190. Attention
191. Steadfast
192. Promises & Words
193. Me, I, Myself
194. Anger
195. Assurance
196. Get Some Sun
197. Interconnectivity
198. Changes
199. That "Church"
200. Commitment
201. Self-Thoughts
202. Speak
203. Tremble!!!
204. "So Loved"
205. Propensity
206. Heal
207. I Smile

208. Slow Motion
209. Wasted
210. Manifest
211. Maximization
212. Pushups
213. Emotions
214. Never Too Sunny
215. Recap
216. Perspective
217. Madly Committed
218. The Fuel
219. Tell Yourself
220. Real
221. No Amount of Money
222. Every Day
223. Thank You
224. Discovered
225. That's It
226. Misplaced
227. Careful Thoughts
228. Mystery
229. In Grace
230. Your Own Brain
231. Distinction
232. In Most Cases
233. Your Own
234. Soulmate?

Whispers from My Mother

235. Dig Deep	261. is it	288. This Time
236. Power	262. Succinctly	289. The Birth
237. Access it	263. The "Hope"	290. Real Actions
238. Reason	264. Faith & Spirituality	291. Listening and Hearing
239. The Entities	265. Be Diligent	292. Opportunities
240. "Never"	266. Little Liliate	293. Can You See!!!
241. P by G	267. Explored Mind	294. Take Time
242. Power of Prosperity	268. Be! Be!! Be!!!	295. 1 on 1
243. Permission	269. Heart & Mind	296. Battles
244. Humility or Ego	270. You Are	297. It Hurts
245. Be Cautious	271. The Good in Everything	298. What Gives
246. Games We Play	272. Best Way	299. Rare
247. If	273. Love-Faith-Hope	300. Move On
248. Address	274. Discretionary Power	301. The World
249. Be It	275. Best Place	302. Deprive Me Not
250. Those Moments	276. Respect your Roots	303. Shift
251. The Future is Present	277. The word "DO"	304. Leadership & Time
252. Neutrality of Consistency	278. Unique	305. Psychological Deficiencies
253. The Phrase	279. Push	306. Some of Us
254. Today's Tomorrow	280. Unseen	307. Recurring
255. Decentralization of Centralization	281. Flow of my Spirit and Consciousness	308. Fighter
256. What's Fear or Favor	282. The Happenings	309. Make it happen
257. Wisdom Sets Us Free	283. A Worlds of Madness	310. Those Moments
258. Wavelengths of Words	284. Don't Be a Fool	311. Desired
259. Its Wholeness	285. Psyche	312. Benjamins & Fools
260. Equality and Equity	286. Scare	313. Freeing Your Mindset
	287. Tree of Knowledge	314. Disciplined Lesson

Whispers from My Mother

315. The Parents
316. Your Truths
317. What's Worth
318. Right Thing
319. Warrants
320. How Dare You
321. Immortality
322. The Focus
323. Say It
324. Hope for You
325. Virtuous
326. "Ka"
327. Best Parts of a Woman
328. The Gray
329. Purpose Fulfilled
330. Doors
331. Distinctive Distinction
332. Ignorance

333. Wise Counsel - pg. 666
334. Success Triggers
335. Mood, Mind, & Power
336. Feeling Jealous?
337. Good Friends are very Rare
338. Living in Reverse
339. Don't Rob Yourself
340. Reverence
341. a Video
342. Untouchable
343. Multilateralism
344. Integrity
345. The Cause
346. Important Core
347. Humility
348. It's okay to cry
349. A World Full of…
350. Unaware vs Aware

351. Too Consumed
352. Don't be Bitter
353. No Exception
354. A Walking Billionaire
355. Receive
356. Now, is The Time
357. The Truth You Seek
358. Why and What
359. Reason Why You are Powerless
360. Difference Between You and I
361. Move in Silence
362. The Heart
363. "Never Give Up"
364. Ready or Just Lucky
365. Climb It
366. Never Forget
Final Words

Whispers from My Mother

Introduction

This book is about thoughts, inspirations, moments, meditations, motivations, wisdom, guidance, liberations, celebrations, struggles, success, life, appreciations, purpose, love, energy, freedom, lessons, laughter, tears, come-backs, determination, knowledge, joy, poems, reflections, happiness and forgiveness.

Take a dose a day of "Whispers from My Mother".

DAY 1

Into Existence

It started with the whispers.

My spirit tingled.

Felt it all over the galaxies.

Echoing through the universe within me.

Loud roar like thousands of lions.

My soul was activated.

Conscious, I became.

It was quiet then a loud explosion ensued.

New birth, new me.

I am, being.

Samuel K. Anderson (Whispers from My Mother)

Whispers from My Mother

Day 2 - The Arrival

I do not know how you got here to this planet: Some got to this

planet:

with both parents,

single parent,

death of both parents on arrival,

sick parents,

rich parents,

poor parents,

roadside/garbage/sewage or fire department delivery.

Probably test tubes

or a surrogate.

No matter your condition of arrival to planet earth. You have an obligation to live a life of legacy. Your energy is needed in this universe that is why you are here. You are important. You matter. The perfect universal flow of energy would be out of balance without your presence. You are an intricate part of the grand plan. Do not let anyone tell you that you don't belong. Those people are the viruses in the universe.

Samuel K. Anderson (Whispers from My Mother)

Whispers from My Mother

DAY 3

The Therapy

Through life's difficult moments:
I find therapy in writing and meditation.
I make something beautiful in the midst of all the storms in life.
What's your therapy? What's your song? What's your story? What's your escape? What's your motivation?
The storm will come, make sure you have a therapeutic plan to remain sane for the moments of stormy waters.

Samuel K. Anderson (Whispers from My Mother)

Whispers from My Mother

DAY 4

This is a Reality Check

I see the very few that are "real" in life's reality test.

My understanding about life has changed.

Those that are there in "real times" of need are those that really matter in my life.

Opinions from unsupportive people that "go ghost" when serious and critical situations happen are irrelevant.

Real actions that are reflective in life's reality are the real things to deal with in life.

Samuel K. Anderson (Whispers from My Mother)

Whispers from My Mother

DAY 5

The Seed of Discord

The most powerful weapon effective to destabilizing the strength, power, intellectual agility, and the union of any friendship, relationship, family, community, institutions, municipality, a state/region or a nation is the seed of discord. Once effectively sowed, you can easily control, manipulate and destroy such people's identity, confidence, knowledge and their very worth. Such distorted people will believe anything outside of themselves.

Samuel K. Anderson (Whispers from My Mother)

Whispers from My Mother

DAY 6

Revolve to Involve to Evolve

One of the many secrets I have personally learned through life is to never settle no matter how undulatingly tortuous my circumstances may display. Rather to revolve to involve to evolve in revolutionary replicability rendered via re-setting, re-focusing, re-evaluating, refreshing, re-strategizing, re-educating and re-charging.

Samuel K. Anderson (Whispers from My Mother)

Whispers from My Mother

DAY 7

The fine polished one

Secretly, everyone wanted to be like him/her

but socially rejected him/her

due to their very own insecurities, miseducation,

and ignorant mindset.

Stride on fine polished one.

Keep on striding.

Samuel K. Anderson (Whispers from My Mother)

Whispers from My Mother

DAY 8

I am Stupendous

My heart

My mind

My body

My sanity

My aura

I am truly stupendous.

Samuel K. Anderson (Whispers from My Mother)

Whispers from My Mother

DAY 9

Ponder!!!

One of the easiest ways
to live life is to laugh at things
you do not understand
but that's also one of the most
foolish ways to live your life.

Samuel K. Anderson (Whispers from My Mother)

Whispers from My Mother

DAY 10

Life's Basic Units

In most life lessons, the most humbling of them all usually comes with the easiest task. We consciously or behaviorally allow pride to sneak its way to our mind and heart until we lose it all or if we are fortunate enough; we encounter a stern warning sign with a second chance. You cannot solidly be versatile in the big things without mastering or bettering the foundations of the smaller things. Every big opportunity, object, obstacle, success, or event constitutes smaller units of its characteristic self.

Samuel K. Anderson (Whispers from My Mother)

Whispers from My Mother

DAY 11 -

The Power in Failure

You encouraged me to try everything

Even when I felt I wasn't good at it.

You will make me feel like a superhuman and then I take a shot at it.

No matter how often I failed,

you still saw me as a winner.

I would tell you that I didn't win,

you always smile and say; silly, you did win.

I never understood the lesson being taught until I was hit with a challenge. I realized that I was built for this, I can do it, I deserve a chance and a shot at it. Success welcomed me with deep embrace, then it all made sense.

Every failure in my life prepared me for this opportunity, thank you mother, for the lesson of "*The Power in failure*".

Samuel K. Anderson (Whispers from My Mother)

Whispers from My Mother

DAY 12 -

The "Going Through"

I believe in that inclination as well.

The "going through" part is very tough.

It hurts,

it's upsetting,

the storm hits hard and right when you think you are

almost out of it;

You get hit with the biggest tsunami.

The truth is: it gets better, it always does.

Samuel K. Anderson (Whispers from My Mother)

Whispers from My Mother

DAY 13

I Am Being

Wisdom flows through me like a fountain of infinite water deriving from a melanated genesis. I live, I breath, I am "being".

I am intricately in uniformity with everything that has existed, is existing and that which is unequivocally yet to come.

It is inexplicably grand, royal and bona fide to all existence and nonexistence. The source of everything revealed to few and anonymous to many due to their spiritual deafness and cavernous tranquilized sleep.

Samuel K. Anderson (Whispers from My Mother)

Whispers from My Mother

DAY 14- Eternal Value

Gain knowledge by investing in your passion then use wisdom to know your true self. Block the lies from the media that doesn't positively feed your passion. Be decisive at the journey, eradicate fear, and appreciate your support group. This will produce power, influence, and wealth. Make sure to build the community that influenced your journey. Be the solution that can induce life, wealth, and health into that community. The package is not where the value resides rather the value is within the package.

You cannot fake value, but you can definitely hide value to encourage the few willing to put in the work to discover the value within the package. Discernment is key to identifying one's value, your value is not in the mirror.

Your value will never die, your value is not buried six feet down the ground, and your value never expires. All you need to do, is to detach yourself from anything that tricks you to believing that your value is the package you see in the mirror. Always remember to be inseparable with anything that sets your soul on fire.

  Samuel K. Anderson (Whispers from My Mother)

Whispers from My Mother

DAY 15

The Strip

Sometimes, God/universe/ or a higher power strip everything from you in order to steer you towards your true purpose.

You may be financially broke.

May get sick.

May lose people you love.

May literally lose everything but your life.

The strip can be scary, but it is meant to draw you closer to God/universe/ or a higher power.

Samuel K. Anderson (Whispers from My Mother)

Whispers from My Mother

DAY 16

Chances vs Doubt

Never doubt yourself more than the chances you give to yourself.

It is simply unfair to doubt your abilities,

who you are, your gifts and tenacity before giving yourself any

chance to succeed. Trust in your abilities to succeed.

Give yourself a chance, trust me,

it's lovely.

Samuel K. Anderson (Whispers from My Mother)

Whispers from My Mother

Day 17

Take Caution

Why is almost everyone around us fake?

Well, it is simply

because we have lost our purpose.

The core to every human being is love.

We all need to find our purpose and then connect it with our core,

a.k.a love.

Samuel K. Anderson (Whispers from My Mother)

Whispers from My Mother

DAY 18

The Interrupters

Fake Life: Oh dear, are you frustrated

Me: I am not frustrated.

I am stating the fact and talking about "real" life.

We all need a reality check from time to time.

I can talk and gossip all night long about someone,

but the fact of the matter is;

do I show up when they really need me?

At your death bed, how many people will truly come to say their goodbyes?

Real people are rare.

Look around your circle/family/friends/colleagues.

Who are the "real" ones, those are the ones that matter.

Samuel K. Anderson (Whispers from My Mother)

Whispers from My Mother

DAY 19

Materialistic and Deceptive World

Having the rapacious propensity for agglomeration with acquisitive conglomeration is a clear indication of a failed bonafide psychological emancipation in a pathological world of illusive dogmatism.

Samuel K. Anderson (Whispers from My Mother)

Whispers from My Mother

DAY 20

Be Extraordinary

Be Powerful.

Be Strong.

Be Extraordinary.

Dare to get to the top. Never give up.

Pain is simply your weakness evaporating from your body.

Demand success and nothing less. Challenge the best.

Never focus on your doubters,

work hard and let the results show.

Samuel K. Anderson (Whispers from My Mother)

Whispers from My Mother

DAY 21

Conversation between Mother & Son

Son: Mother, share with me; who is the right woman for me?

Mother: A queen with a brain, proper etiquette, raised right by her parents and knows how to cook. Make sure you help her in the kitchen from time to time; that's a unique way to bond.

Samuel K. Anderson (Whispers from My Mother)

Whispers from My Mother

DAY 22

Gift of Loyalty

The best gift to give anyone is loyalty.

If there is loyalty, then love can never be questioned.

Right when loyalty is lost,

trust and believe that the love is long gone.

Loyalty is the root of love.

Samuel K. Anderson (Whispers from My Mother)

Whispers from My Mother

DAY 23

Love Never Stops

Explosions of peace, happiness, love and appreciation.

Never stop loving who you are and showing love to others around you.

Love never stops.

It's sometimes redirected towards a different force of attraction.

Burst into peace, happiness, love and appreciation every day.

Samuel K. Anderson (Whispers from My Mother)

Whispers from My Mother

DAY 24

Deeply Rooted

Always stay true to yourself and

never compromise your values to anyone or any influence.

Be deeply rooted in your values,

if you want to go far in life.

Samuel K. Anderson (Whispers from My Mother)

Whispers from My Mother

DAY 25

Say this Repetitively to Yourself

Stupendously stupefied by God's infinite prowess of unmatched providence channeling my extraordinary human dignity.

Samuel K. Anderson (Whispers from My Mother)

Whispers from My Mother

DAY 26

Diversions

We accept so many things we know nothing about - ignorance is a terrible disease.

Education is the key to knowledge and by knowledge we take wise steps to stand for what is right and true.

Pick up a book, read something, execute a research, travel to get to know the world around you with its diverse cultures and people.

Don't rely on the media, 99.99% of the information is pure diversion.

Samuel K. Anderson (Whispers from My Mother)

Whispers from My Mother

DAY 27

Upside Down

We've turned this world into an acceptable illusion that constitutes cyclical political tricks, racial separation, socio-economic classification, deceptive chromoluminarism of religious euphoria, intellectual and psychological daylight robbery of the human consciousness.

Dark diversion of what it's supposed to be; which is oneness of all humanity.

To clear this illusion is for all of us to renew our mind (which sees much deeper to the core) and to not just see things with our eyes (peripheral) - only then will we be able to know, acknowledge and stand together to accomplish the very simple hidden truth that all humans are biologically, spiritually and luminously equal.

Samuel K. Anderson (Whispers from My Mother)

Whispers from My Mother

Day 28

It's a Beautiful Day

It's a beautiful day, first:

Smile.

Good!!!

Relax.

Focus.

You are winning.

Always think and stay positive.

Most importantly, control your internal energy.

Have a terrific day, smile; there you go.

Samuel K. Anderson (Whispers from My Mother)

Whispers from My Mother

DAY 29

Be Strong

I am pushing myself and doing everything ethically possible to succeed.

Life has met me head-on with its greatest challenge,

yet I remain strong, determined and hopeful

as I do what I need to do to turn things around.

Samuel K. Anderson (Whispers from My Mother)

Whispers from My Mother

DAY 30

On Common Sense, Knowledge & Wisdom

In my candid logic of reasoning, common sense and wisdom is far greater than knowledge; in that, knowledge can be manipulated and controlled but wisdom always reign supreme.

Samuel K. Anderson (Whispers from My Mother)

Whispers from My Mother

DAY 31

Aspirations

Never be intimidated or timid about your aspirations.

Push yourself harder.

Do not focus on the difficult situations/conditions/circumstances.

Rather, focus on the possibilities and the opportunities within your circumstance.

Samuel K. Anderson (Whispers from My Mother)

Whispers from My Mother

DAY 32

The Lesson

One thing I have learned in life is that,

forgiveness feels so good.

It's such a powerful feeling to be able to forgive yourself and others

that might have wronged you.

Vengeance, anger, and hate are fast ways to destroy all the

possibilities of a better tomorrow.

Forgiveness is stress free.

Forgiveness is life.

Forgiveness is wealth.

Forgiveness is everything.

Samuel Kwabena Anderson (Whispers from My Mother)

Whispers from My Mother

DAY 33

Intellectual Swag

Let them hate all they want,

just smile,

keep calm and

kill them with your intellectual agility.

Yes, that intellectual swag.

Samuel Kwabena Anderson (Whispers from My Mother)

Whispers from My Mother

DAY 34

Sunken Place Miracle

I see you.

I see what you have been going through.

Your challenges in life will never be in vain.

Keep the faith, keep pushing through.

Sometimes, you feel like there's no way out. The pain, the heart breaks, the failures, the rejections, the losses, the darkness and the sunken places.

You are not meant to be stuck in there, you are meant to go through it and come out victorious.

Your life's story today will be someone else's salvation tomorrow.

Samuel Kwabena Anderson (Whispers from My Mother)

Whispers from My Mother

DAY 35

The Desire

It's an amazing thing to research and to learn about the hidden treasures while unlearning all the lies we have been taught about who we are as a people.

Pick up a book.

Execute a research.

Study about the past.

Learn from the present.

Know who you are, your roots.

Build for a better and brighter future, one that posterity will forever be thankful and grateful for its establishment.

It all begins with a desire and determination to unlearn everything in order to relearn the facts hidden from our world.

Samuel Kwabena Anderson (Whispers from My Mother)

Whispers from My Mother

DAY 36

Introspective Affirmation

I am very impressive.

I am full of brilliance.

I am full of life and passion.

I am glad to see "Me" shine like the king/queen that I am.

Thanks for being such an exceptional human being.

Never forget who you are,

Yes, "Me"; my one and only true self.

Samuel Kwabena Anderson (Whispers from My Mother)

Whispers from My Mother

DAY 37

Common Sense Deciphering

If you believe in the existence of any spiritual entity or the devil however criticize others who believe in God;
then you are basically not on the path of philosophy, wisdom, or spirituality.

Who has seen God?

Who has seen the devil?

Who has seen "fear"?

Who has seen "love"?

None of these entities/energies are seen
yet, we all feel "loved", "afraid", as well as believe in "love" and expressions of "fear".

If one is imaginary, then; are all not imaginary?

Your acceptance of one over the other doesn't make any of them nonexistent.

Samuel Kwabena Anderson (Whispers from My Mother)

Whispers from My Mother

DAY 38

The Waiting Phase

One of the tempting parts of life's journey is the "waiting phase". The "waiting phase" could hurt our ego, pride and relationship. It makes you feel like giving up. You question even if it's worth it. Sometimes you wonder if you are good enough. The "waiting phase" can be brutal especially when you feel like you have given all you've got but still all you hear is "no", "decline", "denied", "rejected", "cancelled".

For those who are able to be consistent, patient or persevere through the "waiting phase"; they're rewarded with their blessings. You will understand after the arrival of the blessings why the "waiting phase" challenged you the way it did.

It is all worth it. Don't give in, keep pushing through the course of life.

Samuel Kwabena Anderson (Whispers from My Mother)

Whispers from My Mother

DAY 39

The Misconception

99% of the world populace misunderstand the logic of love. Most people are too deep in delusion that the simplest truth is missed for massive lies. Hence, more suffering is released upon the world swimming in chaos, insatiability, and grotesque narratives of hate for one another which will lead to an eventual destruction of mankind.

Samuel Kwabena Anderson (Whispers from My Mother)

Whispers from My Mother

DAY 40

Conscious Reminiscing

Common sense precedes any man-made law or constitution. In that, humans came together and applied common sense in writing the laws of a community, nation or mankind. These laws can be amended by the application of common sense when needed. When common sense is enforced, the most complicated things in life are simplified.

Samuel Kwabena Anderson (Whispers from My Mother)

Whispers from My Mother

DAY 41

The Gist

Sometimes we may get distracted while pursuing the goal/purpose. It is human nature for that to happen, do not beat yourself up. Discipline your mind to stay determined to the journey. Stay focus through the realms of perseverance. For it is only then would you be able to accomplish your goals/purpose in life.

Samuel Kwabena Anderson (Whispers from My Mother)

Whispers from My Mother

DAY 42

Your Decision, Your Choice

The beauty of life's journey under the sun is that, we all have 365 solid days annually (366 days with a leap year).

We can feel overwhelmed, give up, push through, plan, execute, succeed, fail-yet-keep-on-trying, stress out, outraged, persistent or victorious.

No matter our decision, the 24 hours contained within a single day does not change, speed up, slow down or expand for anyone.

We all have the power in freedom to choose how we use our 365/366 days. At the end of it all, we have no one to blame but ourselves.

Samuel Kwabena Anderson (Whispers from My Mother)

Whispers from My Mother

DAY 43

The Face Off

Past is not past. There is no present without its past. To correct things in present time; we need to learn, understand and know the past in order to not repeat it. Your past demons will forever torture and haunt you. You will always be on the run, paranoid and causing more havoc to everything/everyone around you unless you face these demons to defeat them as a resolution. To ignore the past is to ignore the present and future.

Samuel Kwabena Anderson (Whispers from My Mother)

Whispers from My Mother

DAY 44

Think Through It

Assumptions are terrible ways to attack people. It's immature to attack people when you lack knowledge about their situation.

Samuel Kwabena Anderson (Whispers from My Mother)

Whispers from My Mother

DAY 45

The Extraordinary

Everybody was created/born to be extra-ordinary. Some of us choose the hard route to be ordinary by starving our mind, body and spirit.

To get back to your original extra-ordinary self. You will need to be aware of the starvation in order to find the right nutrients to feed your mind, body and spirit.

Samuel Kwabena Anderson (Whispers from My Mother)

Whispers from My Mother

DAY 46
We Are Water

Your body contains about 70% of water. You refill your body with water/liquid whenever the 70% drops causing thirst. Together we are mainly water in a bodysuit. Remember the potter and the clay?

W--------We

A---------Are

T---------The

E-----Eternal

R------Realm

Water freezes, vaporizes, boils, cools, takes the shape of the object contained in it. Water is phenomenal. Water easily transforms from one state to another. We are water.

Samuel Kwabena Anderson (Whispers from My Mother)

Whispers from My Mother

DAY 47

The Solution

If you have a problem with facts

then you are the problem.

Samuel Kwabena Anderson (Whispers from My Mother)

DAY 48

Keep Growing

It's easy to be deceived as much as it is to be consciously lost and unaware; it goes hand in hand. There's a slim line between conscious and unconscious; you ought to continuously dig, research, study and grow.

Samuel K. Anderson (Whispers from My Mother)

Whispers from My Mother

Day 49

Greatness

Every greatness is tested with an opposite force as powerful (if not more) as the force of the greatness. Some greatness fall just once as others fall multiple times; the apex of it all is the ability of the said greatness to rise through every opposing force.

Greatness goes through rejections, defeats, torture, isolation, loneliness, humiliations, mockery, deception, pain, and fear. Greatness is your ability to come out tougher, better, finite, exceptional yet humble and graceful to all the lessons taught by the journey.

Samuel Kwabena Anderson (Whispers from My Mother)

Whispers from My Mother

DAY 50

The Truth

The TRUTH is the surest way to connect daily with the universe.

T-----Transmitting

R---------Revealed

U----------Universe

T------------------To

H---------Humanity

Embrace the truth, stick with the truth and walk daily with the truth.

Samuel K. Anderson (Whispers from My Mother)

Whispers from My Mother

DAY 51

Simplistic Meaning

Being materialistically greedy is clear indication that you have not attain true mental freedom in this deceptive world.

Samuel K. Anderson (Whispers from My Mother)

Whispers from My Mother

DAY 52

"Exit In" – "Exit Out"

It is important to exude xenial intelligence to aid our universal transformation as human beings.

Hence, "EXIT in" and "EXIT out" are all part of the universal coordinations of unity and oneness.

E = Exude

X = Xenial

I = Intelligent

T = Transformation

As you "EXIT in" and "EXIT out" in your daily life; make sure to Exude Xenial Intelligence through Transformation.

Samuel K. Anderson (Whispers from My Mother)

Whispers from My Mother

DAY 53

Everything Changed

You came into my life with a smile.

Behind that smile was your true self.

So many changes all around us.

The lows, the darkness, the tsunamis, the fears, the earthquakes, the headaches and all the doubts.

Why in heavens name did I open myself to you?

Because, you are my best friend, my love and a solid partner in this journey.

I am glad that we both decided to welcome each other.

Now, our lives are nothing short of utmost actualizations.

Samuel K. Anderson (Whispers from My Mother)

Whispers from My Mother

DAY 54

Today

Today,

decide to be happy.

How?

Good, look in the mirror.

Have a stare for 60 seconds.

Now, that's all you need to decide to be happy.

Samuel K. Anderson (Whispers from My Mother)

Whispers from My Mother

DAY 55 -

Stability Vs Quick Rising

Strategically,

I will take stability over quick rising

Stability is grounded with solid foundation.

To every quick rising there is high probability of a hard fall.

Samuel K. Anderson (Whispers from My Mother)

Whispers from My Mother

DAY 56

Phases

Your strength and durability

are tested at every

phase of life that

requires perseverance.

Samuel K. Anderson (Whispers from My Mother)

Whispers from My Mother

DAY 57

I Am a god

I am a god!

Yes, I am a god.

How? Why? Because, I am a "god" product of "The God"

We are all gods with specific responsibilities under the sun.

Some are lost gods with lost identities trying and searching to identify their purpose and being.

The "god" can never be greater than "The God"

For it is out of the existence of "The God" that the "god" exists.

A lost god will struggle to identify with "The God" unless the lost god finds his/her "purpose" of existence in direct relation to "The God".

"The God" is everything.

I am then an energy

I am a force

I am a spirit

I am a god.
 Samuel K. Anderson (Whispers from My Mother)

Whispers from My Mother

DAY 58

Knowledge is Freedom

Knowledge doesn't hurt anyone,
it just releases us from intellectual imprisonment.

Knowledge is the first step to gaining wisdom.
Knowledge can be falsified; some are rare and true.
Test every knowledge to find which constitutes the truth.
Seek knowledge daily. It's necessary to pursue knowledge if you truly want to be free.

Samuel K. Anderson (Whispers from My Mother)

Whispers from My Mother

DAY 59

Don't Clog Your Energy

Every day comes with its own challenges.

Some are subtle,

others are aggressive.

Remember to always flush out,

brush off and wash off impurities that

may clog your energy.

Samuel K. Anderson (Whispers from My Mother)

Whispers from My Mother

DAY 60

Confidence

Confidence is a key ingredient to success.

Your confidence will be tested by opposing forces.

The strength and level of your confidence would be vital to how far you go in life.

Can you keep on going when no one believes in you?

Would you give up when even your closest friends, family and sometimes your partner doesn't side with the journey?

Your confidence can make or break you.

Build your confidence up every day. If you believe in what you are doing, then no matter the objection; you ought to make sure to keep on pushing for your goal.

Samuel K. Anderson (Whispers from My Mother)

Whispers from My Mother

DAY 61

Reflections

Your body, your material possessions, your family, friends and loved ones, are all important on this physical planet. You have both good and bad memories of them.

You drive in all the flashy cars. Invest in all the high yield investments and secure numerous real estate businesses and properties worldwide.

Your body is in shape, smooth and radiant skin. Looking elegant and sophisticated in all your clothing.

Family and friends party with you, help spend your wealth and enjoy your material accomplishments.

Rhetorically, how well are you investing in your spirit and consciousness? Your actual wealth is your spiritual health. This is the most important part of your entire being.

We were all born naked with only our spirit and consciousness.

We will all exit this world the same way we entered at birth.

Make sure your spirit is right, make sure your consciousness is fed with enlightenment to achieve its fullness. You will forever be a spirit being.

Connect, meditate, invest, exercise, feed and cherish your spiritual wellbeing.

Samuel K. Anderson (Whispers from My Mother)

Whispers from My Mother

DAY 62 - The Truth is Timeless

Profess the truth as the truth without fear or favor.
Keep the truth as true and never compromise the truth to be untrue just to gain favor with a lair.

Stand "for" and "with" the truth as the truth.
For it is only in that will you gain absolute freedom of consciousness.

Stick with the truth.
Sit with the truth.
Walk with the truth.
Hold on tight to the truth.
Sacrifice for the truth.
Proclaim the truth till the last drop of oxygen escape your lungs.
The truth will remain the truth no matter how heavy the smear of lies cast upon it.
The truth shall and will always prevail;
because the truth is timeless.

Samuel K. Anderson (Whispers from My Mother)

Whispers from My Mother

DAY 63

Success is Birthed

Sometimes you need to do exactly what you don't want to do. Doing this will cause friction. Friction is needed to cause movement. With consistent progression, success is birthed.

Samuel K. Anderson (Whispers from My Mother)

Whispers from My Mother

DAY 64

S.O.A.P

Pessimism is the root of doubt. The best way to turn pessimism is to train your mind to be optimistic. Optimism puts you a step closer to your desired aspiration. Through the spirit of optimism, be determined to put Success Over Any Pessimism.

Success Over Any Pessimism should be your anthem for today and possibly the rest of your life. Whenever you use or see S.O.A.P, make sure to think of Success Over Any Pessimism.

Samuel K. Anderson (Whispers from My Mother)

Whispers from My Mother

DAY 65

Thankful & Blessed

Blessings are all around me.

Blessings are everywhere I go.

Blessings follow me in everything I do.

Blessings to every human.

Blessings to those that bless me and are always there for me.

Thankful for my life.

Thankful for the family, friends and love ones.

Thankful to all the showers of blessings from *The Most High*.

I am indeed thankful and blessed.

What can I say?

How can I repay?

All I can say and do is to be thankful and appreciate all the blessings.

Be Positive. Be Mindful. Be Humble. Be Blessed. Be Thankful.

Samuel K. Anderson (Whispers from My Mother)

Whispers from My Mother

DAY 66

Edification

Edify yourself with the right things.

Take care of yourself daily.

Seek wisdom, knowledge, love and grace.

You have total control in what you absorb.

Make sure you are drinking from the fountain of purified consciousness, spirituality and balance.

Edification through sanctification is paramount to self-actualization in both physical and spiritual realm of your being.

Samuel K. Anderson (Whispers from My Mother)

Whispers from My Mother

DAY 67

Inspiration

What's your inspiration?

What's your goal?

What drives you?

What makes you the best version of yourself?

What keeps you going?

You ought to identify that "thing".

We all have it in us.

It's your purpose.

It's your birthright.

It's your center of existence.

Blessed is the one who finds his/her inspiration for he/she has found his/her birth gem.

Samuel K. Anderson (Whispers from My Mother)

Whispers from My Mother

DAY 68 - Value

What is "value" in your world?

Is it about the money, cars, planes, houses, or material things?

"Value" is very powerful; more powerful than money.

Money is useless without "Value".

Money either gains or loses its "Value" depending on who grants a set "Value" to the money. How do you value yourself?

How do you value the people in your life?

How do you value love, life, commitment, and all the priceless things in life?

Reminisce to have a self-introspection of your "Value" throughout the years to date.

You pick and choose what to grant "Value" to in your life.

Nothing is of "Value" until a "Value" is placed in/on it.

Your "Value" does not change as a human regardless of your awareness or unawareness of it. See your "Value" and walk in all grace, love, confidence and humility to acquire what has always been yours right from birth.

Samuel K. Anderson (Whispers from My Mother)

# Whispers from My Mother

DAY 69

Beware

Fools are simply arrogant. Arrogance breeds ignorance which leads to a shameful fall.

Samuel K. Anderson (Whispers from My Mother)

# Day 70

Mindset

When you fall,

make sure; you do not go into hiding.

Do not be ashamed of your failures.

Do not run away from the issues that caused your fall

rather, face those issues head-on.

Be accountable for what you did right and wrong.

Learn from both sides.

Prepare yourself for a better comeback.

Samuel K. Anderson (Whispers from My Mother)

Whispers from My Mother

DAY 71

The Power of Listening

In a world of chaos, so much distractions and noise;

try your utmost best to listen.

Sometimes, that's all you have to do; just listen.

Listen to your love ones.

Listen to yourself.

Listen to nature and its beautiful sounds and inspirations.

Listen to what's happening around you.

Try to stay away from any interruptions.

Do not be the interrupter either.

Just breath and listen.

Samuel K. Anderson (Whispers from My Mother)

Whispers from My Mother

DAY 72

May I Never Forget

My source is *The Most High*.

My origin is of *The Most High*.

On earth just for a moment.

I am an eternal being.

I live forever and ever.

May I never forget my true source of existence.

Earthly Time has *no* bound on me.

Samuel K. Anderson (Whispers from My Mother)

Whispers from My Mother

DAY 73

Root

For you to thoroughly comprehend the subject matter of a specific topic, name, people or culture is for you to gain a strong hold of the subject matter's etymological anthropology.

Samuel K. Anderson (Whispers from My Mother)

DAY 74

Conscious Awakening

To consciously wake up from your unconscious comatose, you have to separate yourself from all the lies you have been fed through a deliberate willingness to starve every distraction propagated by indiscipline, misguide, and miseducated emotions.

Samuel K. Anderson (Whispers from My Mother)

Whispers from My Mother

DAY 75

Treasure

The truth is like a rare treasure hidden from the masses as lies are given out as everyday dosage.

Samuel K. Anderson (Whispers from My Mother)

DAY 76

Trading Places

Never sacrifice something that gives you joy and purpose for something guaranteed for a quick satisfaction.

Samuel K. Anderson (Whispers from My Mother)

Whispers from My Mother

DAY 77

Life Unknown

Some threats are obvious and avoidable, but the real threat to life is to continuously live a life full of denial.

Samuel K. Anderson (Whispers from My Mother)

Whispers from My Mother

DAY 78

Bigger, Better, Greater

Every time you think about fear in life,

know that it is a tactic to keep you within

your comfort zones.

Dare to expand, refine, progress,

evolve, mature, and advance to your next level.

Samuel K. Anderson (Whispers from My Mother)

Whispers from My Mother

Day 79

Snap Out

Snap out of your illusions.

Snap out of your sleep.

Snap out of your self-inflicted

mental slavery. Regardless of who

deceived or forced you to take the pill

of illusion that caused your tranquilized sleep;

you have the power to decide to set yourself free.

Samuel K. Anderson (Whispers from My Mother)

Whispers from My Mother

DAY 80

Aha!!

If you have life, be grateful.

If you have life and good health,

be exceedingly grateful.

The rest of the things you need in life,

will fall in place for you; just believe and

act on it without fear.

Samuel K. Anderson (Whispers from My Mother)

Whispers from My Mother

DAY 81

It Could Burn

One of the most painful things
in life is to tirelessly explain and prove
yourself to the ones you love only to find out
that they do not give a dime about you.
That burns.

(Samuel K. Anderson (Whispers from My Mother)

Whispers from My Mother

DAY 82

Good Energy

To love yourself is to embrace discipline,

to embrace discipline is to be astute,

to be astute is to be diplomatic,

to be diplomatic is to be lighthearted,

to be lighthearted is to be amour propre.

Samuel K. Anderson (Whispers from My Mother)

Whispers from My Mother

DAY 83

Perspective

In life, we all have that choice,

what will you choose?

A "*loss*" or "*learn*" from it.

Succeed and help others to also succeed.

Leave a legacy and learn every day.

I see no way ahead then I will make sure to create one.

Perspective influences your thoughts

which in turn fuels your mindset.

Samuel K. Anderson (Whispers from My Mother)

Whispers from My Mother

DAY 84

Resist Fear

Fear will easily destroy your world
before it destroys your life.
This world will fail because we
have allowed fear to be a reason
to destroy each other regardless of
our differences and indifferences.

Samuel K. Anderson (Whispers from My Mother)

Whispers from My Mother

DAY 85

The highs, The lows, The in-betweens

Sometimes, I feel high.

Sometimes, I feel low.

Other times, I feel in-between.

I have learned to always remain calm

within myself.

To not waiver no matter the strength of the storm.

Because, it always gets better.

After all, everything is cyclical under the sun.

Celebrate in your highs.

Learn in yours lows.

Appreciate in your in-betweens.

Samuel K. Anderson (Whispers from My Mother)

Day 86

Welcome it All

Never deny an entry to the inspirations

that come knocking at the door

of your consciousness.

Welcome them with open arms.

Figure out why they came to you

and put them into perspective.

Samuel K. Anderson (Whispers from My Mother)

Whispers from My Mother

DAY 87

Unexpectedly Expected

Sometimes the greatest of our breakthroughs come from areas of least expectations. This is the unexpectedly expected.

Samuel K. Anderson (Whispers from My Mother)

Whispers from My Mother

DAY 88

You Fall to Rise

You don't fall to be miserable.

You fall to rise in grace and strength.

Samuel K. Anderson (Whispers from My Mother)

Whispers from My Mother

DAY 89

Conscious Energy

Everything in existence to the conscious mind of human beings is a small portion of everything in its existence on the grand scheme.

Samuel K. Anderson (Whispers from My Mother)

Whispers from My Mother

DAY 90

Choose to Challenge Yourself

If you ever have the option to choose

between easy and challenging route to success.

I hope that you do not choose the easy

way out.

Life is full of tests. You will be tested

sooner or later. Strive to choose a challenging

route if you have the chance to choose.

Challenge yourself and make it worth it.

Samuel K. Anderson (Whispers from My Mother)

Whispers from My Mother

DAY 91

The Art of Giving Up

Why do we give up?

In some cases, it's due to fear.

It most cases, it's due to disinterest.

There are some people that are not afraid

to fail however there are lot of people

with disinterest in what they do.

When you are interested, you will not be

crippled by fear. You will make it happen.

The art to giving up has more to do with disinterest

than with being afraid.

Samuel K. Anderson (Whispers from My Mother)

Whispers from My Mother

DAY 92

The Key to Unlock

Remove every cataract that obstructs your flow of progress.

Break the chain that restrain your passion.

Invest heavily in your mind. The power to full liberation is strongly dependent on the muscle strengths of your mind.

Samuel K. Anderson (Whispers from My Mother)

Whispers from My Mother

DAY 93

Fossilization by Petrification

When you set the goal so high.

You are definitely going to be petrified

and that's okay. You may even think about

doing a 180 turn around to give it all up;

that feeling is okay too.

However, under no circumstance should

fossilization by petrification engulf your aspirations.

Keep the accelerator in place and keep driving forward.

Samuel K. Anderson (Whispers from My Mother)

Whispers from My Mother

DAY 94

Moments of Vulnerabilities

In the midst of vulnerability,

lies one of your greatest opportunities

to embrace your wholeness and your

capability to sprang into your ultimate

self.

Samuel K. Anderson (Whispers from My Mother)

Whispers from My Mother

DAY 95

Illusion of Time

Time doesn't run out.

Do not fall for the pressure of time.

Time is an illusion.

There are not twelve months in a year.

Some civilizations have ten months; others have thirteen.

Do not fall for the pressure rather push for your passion.

What makes you free, that's your light and that's how you are supposed to move in this space and moment.

Samuel K. Anderson (Whispers from My Mother)

Whispers from My Mother

DAY 96

The Love Factor

Love is one of the most miscommunicated expressions, yet its form is very simplistic.

What is to love, to cherish and to hold?

What is love without the freedom of living?

Love is the core to our existence, the air for our very survival.

To comprehend love is to comprehend ourselves. To exercise love is to exercise freedom of parties involved without fear or favor. Love is very precious, it's worth dying for yet the world misunderstands and misinterprets its fulness.

Samuel K. Anderson (Whispers from My Mother)

Whispers from My Mother

DAY 97

Messengers

We are all here on a mission. Every single one of you including all living things.

We all have platforms to deliver our message and services regardless of how small or big our platforms may be.

Our mission begins with a heartbeat right when the electronic energy successfully strikes the diploid cell, known as zygote.

Some missions are prematurely terminated by the mother ship housing the messenger(s). The mission and the message are delivered consciously or unconsciously from the homeless, the rich, the middle class, the poor, the brave, the timid, the deceiver, the peace keeper, the warmonger, the spiritual ones, the soil mixing organisms and the list goes on.

When it's all said and done, we are terminated from this physical dimension to our true self; spiritual beings.

Samuel K. Anderson (Whispers from My Mother)

Whispers from My Mother

DAY 98

It's All About Service

Service for one another is our bread and butter.

Leadership is service to the followers and the followers are in service of the leaders.

Everything we do is wrapped around the offering of service to either ourselves or to one another. We are all people of service. The question is, how are you choosing to execute your service in this moment and time of your physical existence.

Samuel K. Anderson (Whispers from My Mother)

Whispers from My Mother

DAY 99

Free

At some point in this life,

we free ourselves from ourselves.

Don't hold yourself captive till the very end.

Samuel K. Anderson (Whispers from My Mother)

DAY 100

Psychological Freedom

One of the best freedoms in this life
is psychological freedom.
The ability to take control of
your conscious self from all the viruses
in this world is definitely one
of the ultimate freedoms in life.

Samuel K. Anderson (Whispers from My Mother)

Whispers from My Mother

DAY 101 - Versatility Mindset

Be aware.

Be alert.

Be resolute.

Be informed.

Be knowledgeable.

Be persistent.

Be daring.

Be a fighter.

Be a believer.

Be resilient.

Be confident and persuasive.

Be brilliant.

Be a repetitive failure.

Be stubbornly determined to bounce back.

Be useful of grit.

Be fearless.

Be adventurous.

Be daring.

Do not be timid or intimidated regardless of your circumstance.
Samuel K. Anderson (Whispers from My Mother)

Whispers from My Mother

DAY 102

Comprennent

Being speechless is also a

means of communication.

Those who understand you

will understand you.

Ceux qui vous comprennent

vous comprendront.

Samuel K. Anderson (Whispers from My Mother)

Whispers from My Mother

DAY 103

Intent of Manifestation

When you try too hard,

usually nothing comes out of it.

The outcome is dependent on what I call,

the intent of manifestation.

Samuel K. Anderson (Whispers from My Mother)

Whispers from My Mother

DAY 104

Special Self

To be special is to be special,

not to be special for someone else;

rather to be special to the special being

of your special self.

Samuel K. Anderson (Whispers from My Mother)

Whispers from My Mother

DAY 105

Ability

We all have the ability.
The ability to use your ability
to attain your abilities is your
ability. The level of your ability
is set by your ability to recognize
your endless abilities.
Hence, the ability of your abilities
is your own ability.

Samuel K. Anderson (Whispers from My Mother)

Whispers from My Mother

DAY 106

You

What you welcome

welcomes you.

So what are you welcoming to welcome you?

Samuel K. Anderson (Whispers from My Mother)

Whispers from My Mother

DAY 107

Infinity

Infinity is not infinity

if you do not think of it

as infinity.

Samuel K. Anderson (Whispers from My Mother)

Whispers from My Mother

DAY 108

Let them flow

Don't doubt yourself.

Let them flow.

The unlimited passion,

drive, actions, dreams, plans,

service, burning desire, fulfillment,

and imaginations.

Let them all flow through you;

absorb them all.

Samuel K. Anderson (Whispers from My Mother)

Whispers from My Mother

DAY 109

Light

The light lights when lit.
Make sure you light your light
to light up all your paths that
need lightning.

Samuel K. Anderson (Whispers from My Mother)

Whispers from My Mother

DAY 110

Aeration of Your Life

Apply aerification from time to time to give yourself some air in order to air out all the tensed unhealthy air constricted within your heart, mind and veins for proper aeration of your life.

Samuel K. Anderson (Whispers from My Mother)

Whispers from My Mother

DAY 111

Spiritually Awakening

Sourcing your source

is to source your source

from within your source.

Samuel K. Anderson (Whispers from My Mother)

Whispers from My Mother

DAY 112

Truce of No Repetition

Within confusion of calamities

lie the portal of peace in

lessons learnt waving a truce

of no repetition.

Lessons unlearned render

repetition of cyclical calamities.

Samuel K. Anderson (Whispers from My Mother)

Whispers from My Mother

DAY 113

Self-Talk

You are not for everyone.

Your dreams are not for everyone.

Your energy is not for everyone.

Your goals, gifts and talents are not for everyone.

You were not created or born for everyone.

Your mission on earth is not for everyone.

Your physical and spiritual consciousness are not for everyone.

So do not live a life that yearns for everyone's approval.

You will be accountable after this life,

it doesn't matter whether you accept it,

believe it or deny it.

Live your life because you are responsible

of your life and will be held accountable for it.

Samuel K. Anderson (Whispers from My Mother)

Whispers from My Mother

DAY 114

The Challenge

Train your mind to see through the impermeable.

Samuel K. Anderson (Whispers from My Mother)

Whispers from My Mother

DAY 115

O.R.A.N.G.E

Ostentatiously Resist Any Negative Gravitational Energy that gravitates towards you.

Feed your body, mind and spirit with all the nutrients in this **ORANGE** daily.

Samuel K. Anderson (Whispers from My Mother)

Whispers from My Mother

Day 116

You Have the Power

Block foolishness and foolish people.

Delete them.

Ignore them.

Mute them.

You have the power to not entertain them.

Samuel K. Anderson (Whispers from My Mother)

Whispers from My Mother

DAY 117

Over stand

Take your time

to understand yourself daily.

Do you over stand?

Good, now let's get to work.

Samuel K. Anderson (Whispers from My Mother)

DAY 118

Get It Going

Don't always try to understand it

before you do it.

Sometimes you have to do it to understand it.

Samuel K. Anderson (Whispers from My Mother)

Whispers from My Mother

Day 119

You Are the Judge

There are more outside voices
than inside voices.
Outside voices are meant to
challenge you.
Inside voices are meant to move
you to take action.
You are the judge.
You decide which voices to grant
justice of relevance.

Samuel K. Anderson (Whispers from My Mother)

Whispers from My Mother

DAY 120

Got It

Give it one more try,

that's how the miracle happens.

Samuel K. Anderson (Whispers from My Mother)

DAY 121

Self- Check

Whenever you catch yourself

making too much noise;

run a quick self-assessment to

see how full or how empty you are

then make a wise decision based on

the outcome of the self-introspection.

Samuel K. Anderson (Whispers from My Mother)

Whispers from My Mother

DAY 122

Read it Again

You can't be a host

to a leech forever

and expect to thrive forever.

Read it again.

Samuel K. Anderson (Whispers from My Mother)

Whispers from My Mother

DAY 123

The Reason

Your nightmares are

continual reminder

to put your mind at ease

and to take control of it.

Samuel K. Anderson (Whispers from My Mother)

Whispers from My Mother

DAY 124

Growth

There is little

to no growth

without some sort

of disagreement.

Samuel K. Anderson (Whispers from My Mother)

Whispers from My Mother

DAY 125

Genius

Don't hesitate to wake the genius in you.

Feed it.

Exercise it.

Pay attention to it.

Above all, give that genius in you a chance

to do what it was meant to do and see what happens.

Samuel K. Anderson (Whispers from My Mother)

Whispers from My Mother

DAY 126

What Do You See?

When you look at a circle

what do you see?

Do you see the space within

the boundaries of the circle or

the limitless space outside the

circle's circumference?

Now, you should know what to do.

Samuel K. Anderson (Whispers from My Mother)

Whispers from My Mother

DAY 127

See Me

I saw you.

You saw me.

We've seen each other,

but did you really see through me

or did you just saw me.

Samuel K. Anderson (Whispers from My Mother)

Whispers from My Mother

DAY 128

Who am I

Look into the mirror.

Now, stare very hard

and deeply into your eyes.

Close your eyes for a second, open them.

What do you see?

Ask yourself, who am I?

Make sure your answer is exactly who you need to be.

Samuel K. Anderson (Whispers from My Mother)

Whispers from My Mother

DAY 129

Addicted to Success

The road to success hurts.

It can hurt your ego.

It will hurt your pride.

It hurts your confidence.

Sometimes, you can even feel

the pain of depression and rage.

That's what makes the destination

worthwhile. Once you have experienced

the adrenaline and mastered maneuverability;

you begin to be so addicted to success that you are

always willing to go through the journey all over again.

Samuel K. Anderson (Whispers from My Mother)

Whispers from My Mother

DAY 130

Regardless

For tomorrow to be better

you ought to start today,

turn on your ignition;

regardless of your momentum.

Samuel K. Anderson (Whispers from My Mother)

Whispers from My Mother

DAY 131

Sunset

The beauty

of the sunset

is the glory

of its shadow.

Samuel K. Anderson (Whispers from My Mother)

Whispers from My Mother

DAY 132

Joyfully

You can live a life

of luxury,

just define your

version of luxury

and live it up joyfully.

Samuel K. Anderson (Whispers from My Mother)

Whispers from My Mother

DAY 133

In It

Contentment of content

is the content of intent

valued in moderation.

Samuel K. Anderson (Whispers from My Mother)

DAY 134

Oblivion

Purposefully purporting your purpose is purpose pretentiously proclaimed which propels into oblivion.

Samuel K. Anderson (Whispers from My Mother)

Whispers from My Mother

DAY 135

Grounded

Prophesying your profession leads to the eventual possession of your profession.

Samuel K. Anderson (Whispers from My Mother)

Whispers from My Mother

DAY 136

Characterize

When it's all said and done,
character will characterize considerable
courtesy of apex received from life,
companions, acquaintances and family.

Samuel K. Anderson (Whispers from My Mother)

Whispers from My Mother

DAY 137

Confide

Confide internally within yourself of all the crippling fears to awaken the confidence within you. Then externally cripple all the obstacles in your way.

Samuel K. Anderson (Whispers from My Mother)

Whispers from My Mother

DAY 138

Codes

In this universe, we have codes that are made specifically for each person. Inside the codes are your individualistic extraordinary significance. There are specific keys for all the codes. Whenever you are ready, just use your keys to unlock your ordained codes to open the doors to your reason of being. Remember, no one can access your codes; if you fail to use these codes before your time on earth expires then you will be buried with these codes.

Use them while you can breathe in and out.

Samuel K. Anderson (Whispers from My Mother)

Whispers from My Mother

DAY 139

Pause to Ponder

The brightness of the sun at its peak in the day is not dependent on the nature of its rise in the morning.

Samuel K. Anderson (Whispers from My Mother)

Whispers from My Mother

DAY 140

Constantly Creating

You are a creator

who needs to keep

on creating.

Your thought of not

being a creator is a

means of creation in itself.

You are constantly creating

consciously or unconsciously.

Samuel K. Anderson (Whispers from My Mother)

Whispers from My Mother

DAY 141 - "Euphoria"

It was a quiet morning, you could hear a feather drop on the floor.
I stare in lost escape as the hand of the clock tick tocks away; revealing to me the immeasurable opportunities in every second of its movement.
Was that time, space and life crunching their precious moments at my pleasure?
Was that a signal of exhibition whispering all the astounding things yet to happen?
Was that time, space and life igniting my much anticipated purpose in this physical realm? Shivers of euphoria transmitting through every inch of my neurons.
I got up from my dazed position to strike at all the endless possibilities that this intimate moment gifted to me.

Samuel K. Anderson (Whispers from My Mother)

Whispers from My Mother

DAY 142

Aspire to Inspire

Be inspired to use your inspiration

to inspire yourself and others

to aspire for greater inspirations

tantamount to catapult yourself

and others to their exponential altitude.

Samuel K. Anderson (Whispers from My Mother)

Whispers from My Mother

DAY 143

Ignorance

The only person responsible
for your ignorance is yourself.
If you read it and do not comprehend it;
maybe you can do yourself a favor
to research to gain some wisdom
about the topic or situation.
Ignorance is a self-inflicting
disease propagated by laziness
that renders into psychological
deception and delusion.

Samuel K. Anderson (Whispers from My Mother)

Whispers from My Mother

DAY 144

Exude

The brightness of

a star does not

depend on its size.

Samuel K. Anderson (Whispers from My Mother)

Whispers from My Mother

Day 145

Conscious Beauty

A conscious beauty doesn't need

to be told that she's conscious or beautiful

in order for her to know.

Know who you are and

be confident with your

distinct persona. Your

aura is your romance to safeguard.

Your king awaits you

beautiful queen.

Samuel K. Anderson (Whispers from My Mother)

Whispers from My Mother

DAY 146

Pondering

Every ethnicity on planet

earth can track its natives.

What's your ethnic group?

Do you know? Why is that?

Let this rhetoric inspire you to start

digging for some answers.

Samuel K. Anderson (Whispers from My Mother)

Whispers from My Mother

DAY 147

Infinite Love

The moon and back

is just the beginning

of my love for you.

What can be!

What will be and

What is yet to come

Are all just a wonder

in my infinite plethora

of love for you.

Come my dear,

Take my hand and

Let's soar into the dimension

of infinite love.

Samuel K. Anderson (Whispers from My Mother)

Whispers from My Mother

DAY 148

Scars

Take a moment to observe

your scars.

Each scar represents a moment,

or a situation in your life.

These scars represent a time

of transitional growth or bitter

lessons. Your scars should be your

motivation to create a better

situation for yourself at present to

the future. Cherish them, appreciate them

and embrace them because those scars

are part of your whole being.

Samuel K. Anderson (Whispers from My Mother)

Whispers from My Mother

DAY 149

Instead

Worrying and complaining cause nothing but stagnation and retrogression. Fix that energy on fixing the situations and building for a better tomorrow.

Samuel K. Anderson (Whispers from My Mother)

Whispers from My Mother

DAY 150

Work It

The hardest part of believing in yourself is the work that accompanies it. The energy needed to believe in yourself is different from the energy needed to get the work done. Make sure you are ready to put in that energy to work to attain what you believe in.

Samuel K. Anderson (Whispers from My Mother)

Whispers from My Mother

DAY 151

Youthful Days

The shortfall of a youth is
to think that everything
last forever. It feels majestic in
youthful days but make sure to
seize those majestic moments to
secure a formidable future of
wisdom, grace, success and awareness.

Samuel K. Anderson (Whispers from My Mother)

Whispers from My Mother

DAY 152

Distractions

Don't be a rough rider
through life's journey.
There are so many warning signs,
sharp curves, red lights, hills and
valleys. Any distraction can cost you
severely. Pay attention to all the warning
signs and make the best decision when it's
time to do so. Make sure you have fun
while on this trip.

Samuel K. Anderson (Whispers from My Mother)

Whispers from My Mother

DAY 153

Trust Me

Trust can test the best

and worst of you.

One of the most telling of

a person's intentions are when

the trust that was once upheld

is broken.

Samuel K. Anderson (Whispers from My Mother)

Whispers from My Mother

DAY 154

It's Yours

Happiness, good health, peace of mind, pure love, heart of joy and a beautiful soul are all pure energies that we decide to either embrace or reject. If you look into your life and you feel empty or missing any of these life energies; just make a conscious decision to attract, embrace and hold on to as many of these positive life-filled energies as possible. It's your choice, your personal decision to make.

Samuel K. Anderson (Whispers from My Mother)

… Whispers from My Mother

DAY 155

Learn through Grace

Show me anyone who enjoys trials or is willing to choose trials over joy and peace of mind. The trails however are part of your spiritual, conscious and physical transitions. As much as we all hate trail times; we should see and learn all the lessons those trial moments present to us. Learn through grace in the midst of your trials to evolve into your powerful self.

Samuel K. Anderson (Whispers from My Mother)

Whispers from My Mother

DAY 156

Time to Progress

Observe babies in their attempt to stand up.

Observe their persistence in taking the first step.

Pay attention to their earnest resistance to give up.

Now, imagine some children deciding to just sit

and cry all day to be picked up instead of pushing

through the complexities involved in taking their

first steps. Think about these things when you

feel stuck in a situation. You have to cause some resistance

in order to produce enough friction to ignite some progress.

You are not stuck; you are just enjoying your long break.

Samuel K. Anderson (Whispers from My Mother)

Whispers from My Mother

DAY 157

Breaks

Descending on a steep slope
requires workable breaks to
prevent possible drastic accident.
Hence, in life; you must make sure
to turn on your breaks of self-control
and self-discipline whenever things get
out of hand to prevent possible damages.

Samuel K. Anderson (Whispers from My Mother)

Whispers from My Mother

DAY 158 "The Secret Code"

The darker you are the stronger the energetic field of attraction. The source of the god-like energy is the Melanin.

You are mocked.

You are discriminated against.

You are tortured. You are wrongfully accused.

You are hated for no reason.

Your natural hair, looks, energy and being are always envied.

Because you are everything, they wish they could be. The source of your melanin is the *Melanated Creator* of all things known and unknown to every creation. You are rare. You are

The Creator's heartbeat. You are a part of the air *The Creator* breathes.

They all feed off of your energy.

Regain your conscious power.

Regain your spiritual power.

Regain your physical power.

Regain your God-ordained melanin.

You already have it. The code is already infused in you.

You are a god directly from God.

You are powerful from the Omnipotent.

You are present from the Omnipresent.

You are conscientious from the Omniscient.

Samuel K. Anderson (Whispers from My Mother)

Whispers from My Mother

DAY 159

Precious Gift

In all clarity, I seem to notice what interests me.
I may not notice everything, yet; I definitely know when to make a statement and when to just keep walking.
Life is too precious to waste mine on useless things.
Keep breathing and keep walking towards your goals.

Samuel K. Anderson (Whispers from My Mother)

Whispers from My Mother

DAY 160

Precision

You cannot grow spiritually without growing physically and consciously.

Samuel K. Anderson (Whispers from My Mother)

Whispers from My Mother

DAY 161

Don't Hide

There are too many books out there.

There are also so many quotes, phrases or sayings out there.

However, none of those compare

to your own story,

your own quotes, phrases or sayings.

So, don't hide these gifts at your

safest hideouts.

Go on and let them out to be a

blessing to those present and

those who are yet to come.

Samuel K. Anderson (Whispers from My Mother)

Whispers from My Mother

DAY 162

Seize the Moments

If you fail to read,

research, study and

dig deeper for answers

then you widely open yourself

to be swayed by those who

seize the moments to read,

research, study and dig deeper.

Samuel K. Anderson (Whispers from My Mother)

Whispers from My Mother

DAY 163

True Image

One of the secret weapons of a mirror is its power to always reflect one's true image no matter the occasion, class or association.

Samuel K. Anderson (Whispers from My Mother)

Whispers from My Mother

DAY 164

Sense of Smell

It can smell terrific.

It can smell neutral,

and it can smell terrible.

It all depends on what

side of the situation you

are on.

May be, we all ought to

get our sense of smell

checked from time to time.

Samuel K. Anderson (Whispers from My Mother)

Whispers from My Mother

DAY 165

Risk

Go all in on taking risk.

Yes, all in as in one hundred percent.

Fail all out, flat out.

Win all out, clean and strong.

Samuel K. Anderson (Whispers from My Mother)

DAY 166

Plan the Plan

Planning your plans to plan well is part of the plan in planning.

Samuel K. Anderson (Whispers from My Mother)

Whispers from My Mother

DAY 167

Common Denominator

What's the common denominator here?

self-esteem

self-defense

self-sufficient

self-knowledge

self-destruction

self-love

self-acknowledgement

self-determination

self-hate

self-pity

The common denominator is "self".

You owe every single right to your self

to live right or to live dragged.

Samuel K. Anderson (Whispers from My Mother)

DAY 168

Strategic

Strategically strategizing the strategies are key to striking home most of the strategic strategies strategized.

Samuel K. Anderson (Whispers from My Mother)

Whispers from My Mother

DAY 169

Gifted

Gifted gifts are
gifts for the gifted.
Use your gifts to
gift your world and
if possible, the whole world.

Samuel K. Anderson (Whispers from My Mother)

Whispers from My Mother

DAY 170

The "*you*" within You

Allow your mind to roam free

through all the infinite possibilities.

Set it free.

Let it fly as high as it can go.

You will be amazed by the places it takes you.

Your mind.

Your world.

Your being.

Your soul.

Your trusted "you" within you.

Samuel K. Anderson (Whispers from My Mother)

Whispers from My Mother

DAY 171

Creative

Creativities of the creative are geared by creative ambitions and thoughts of the creator.

Samuel K. Anderson (Whispers from My Mother)

DAY 172

Insecurities

One's acknowledgement of impossibility is merely an exposure of one's insecurities permeating through his own doubts, fears, denials, incompetence and lack of self-knowledge.

Samuel K. Anderson (Whispers from My Mother)

Whispers from My Mother

DAY 173

Get It Done

Show me what you desire to accomplish.

List the steps you have already taken.

None? Well, get started.

Few but haven't worked?

Well, try harder;

Use different approach.

Samuel K. Anderson (Whispers from My Mother)

DAY 174

Never Again

Doubtfulness is the power you give to your destructive self.

Samuel K. Anderson (Whispers from My Mother)

Whispers from My Mother

DAY 175

Word.

There is absolutely no love without self-love. You can never change that phenomenon.

Samuel K. Anderson (Whispers from My Mother)

DAY 176

Clearheaded

Sufficiency is the efficiency of contentment.

Samuel K. Anderson (Whispers from My Mother)

Whispers from My Mother

DAY 177

Choose Peace

We are all one decision away from another world war outbreak. Greed and incompetent leadership will sink at least one third of the human populace.

Samuel K. Anderson (Whispers from My Mother)

Whispers from My Mother

DAY 178

Clarity in Confusion

There can exist so much clarity in confusion and so much confusion in clarity. It all depends on the agility of the individual in question. Understand that without the presence of confusion; there is little to no desire to seek clarity.

Samuel K. Anderson (Whispers from My Mother)

Whispers from My Mother

Day 179

The Beauty in Humility

We were all ignorant at one point. The beauty in humility is its ability of admittance to ignorance and to gradually replace ignorance with knowledge. Those who hold on long enough to humility eventually gain wisdom through diverse acquired knowledge.

Samuel K. Anderson (Whispers from My Mother)

Whispers from My Mother

DAY 180

You Ready?

When you are at the
lowest of your lows.
You have the choice to
decide on how long you
want to stay there or how
quick you desire to get right
back up.

Samuel K. Anderson (Whispers from My Mother)

Whispers from My Mother

DAY 181

Greater and Lesser selves

Within each one of us lies greater
and lesser selves of yourself.
Lesser people decided to choose
their lesser selves instead of their greater self.
Great people decided to choose
their greater selves instead of their lesser selves.
The work, discipline, mindset, accountability
and determination needed to become
either self is dependent upon which self
you decide to choose.
These choices are found within your
reason of being; your purpose in your
existence.

Samuel K. Anderson (Whispers from My Mother)

Whispers from My Mother

DAY 182

Inward Outward

Invest in yourself and your true self will invest in your outward environment. Investing in yourself will yield the needed qualities already existing within you to illuminate your environment both internally and externally.

Samuel K. Anderson (Whispers from My Mother)

DAY 183

Unknown Known

To know the unknown

is to unknow what you know

and to re-know all the unknowns.

Samuel K. Anderson (Whispers from My Mother)

Whispers from My Mother

DAY 184

Profound

So long as you are alive
regardless of your age with the
obvious exception of children who
have not reached the age of consciousness;
you have every right to dream big and the
ability to become whatever you have
always desire to become at any time in your life.

Samuel K. Anderson (Whispers from My Mother)

Whispers from My Mother

DAY 185

Dare

Show me all those
that are failing in life
and I will show you
what they are doing right.

Samuel K. Anderson (Whispers from My Mother)

DAY 186

Bold Faith

You can never become

what you don't believe.

It will definitely never

happen unless you have

the zeal, the audacity and

the intentions to become what

you believe of becoming.

Samuel K. Anderson (Whispers from My Mother)

Whispers from My Mother

DAY 187

Different

Our world seems to
almost always easily
embrace fraudsters
faster than people
of true value and dignity.
Try your utmost best to
be sanctified differently.

Samuel K. Anderson (Whispers from My Mother)

Whispers from My Mother

DAY 188

Audacity Decoded

God's audacity propels human's audacity. Human's audacity responds to God's audacity. The propensity of human's audacity manifestations is dependent on the propensity of "God-like" attributes sustained and awakened within us.

Samuel K. Anderson (Whispers from My Mother)

Whispers from My Mother

DAY 189

Good

The good in
the goods
are the goods
in the good.

Samuel K. Anderson (Whispers from My Mother)

Whispers from My Mother

DAY 190

Attention

The fact that the shoe may fit comfortably doesn't necessarily mean it's for you.

Samuel K. Anderson (Whispers from My Mother)

: Whispers from My Mother

DAY 191

Steadfast

Encourage yourself to never discourage yourself whenever you need some encouragements.

Samuel K. Anderson (Whispers from My Mother)

Whispers from My Mother

DAY 192

Promises & Words

Adulteration of your promises or words in any given situation regardless of its magnitude are pure indications of your promiscuous intentions that eventually wear off the marriage holding the constituents of the circumstances together.

Samuel K. Anderson (Whispers from My Mother)

Whispers from My Mother

DAY 193

Me, I, Myself

Make sure to
introduce yourself
to your main self
to make sure that
yourself knows your
main self.

Samuel K. Anderson (Whispers from My Mother)

Whispers from My Mother

DAY 194

Anger

No human being can confidently claim to never have been angry. When you get angry just try your best to think about your favorite person or favorite place in your life; that's a workable trick for me.

Samuel K. Anderson (Whispers from My Mother)

Whispers from My Mother

DAY 195

Assurance

Show me who will pass on a certified assurance and I will show you a foolish person.

Samuel K. Anderson (Whispers from My Mother)

Whispers from My Mother

DAY 196

Get Some Sun

Bitterness may come to some people as a safe zone to nurture their bitter experiences. No matter how insanely safe you may feel; the remedy is to free yourself from the grips of bitterness to allow some sun into your life.

Samuel K. Anderson (Whispers from My Mother)

Whispers from My Mother

Day 197

Interconnectivity

We all indirectly

or directly motivate

each other positively

or negatively on a

conscious or unconscious

equilibrium propelled by

the basic units of our

intertwined interconnectivity.

Samuel K. Anderson (Whispers from My Mother)

Whispers from My Mother

DAY 198

Changes

Changes are key

to every living

organism's growth.

Allow yourself to adapt

"<u>through</u>" and "<u>to</u>" things,

environments, situations,

relationships and opportunities.

Samuel K. Anderson (Whispers from My Mother)

Whispers from My Mother

DAY 199

That "Church"

Let's come together

to form a church of

entrepreneurs that look

out for each other's

mega opening and expansion.

This is the kind of church

I want to be a part of.

Let's get it started.

Samuel K. Anderson (Whispers from My Mother)

Whispers from My Mother

DAY 200

Commitment

Communication is very important in every relationship. Understanding is pivotal in every communication. However, the most important piece of effective communication is nothing less from commitment. One can communicate effectively with the parties involved having a crystal clear understanding but if there is no commitment then what's communicated is useless to accomplishing its purpose.

Samuel K. Anderson (Whispers from My Mother)

Whispers from My Mother

DAY 201

Self-Thoughts

There is absolutely nothing wrong with almost always thinking about yourself. That's actually brilliant; however, make sure that you are thinking good of yourself and allow that good vibe thoughts and acts to flow through the environment you reside.

Samuel. K. Anderson (Whispers from My Mother)

Whispers from My Mother

DAY 202

Speak

If you have the power to say anything to yourself and the power to become anything you choose to become then why do you decide to choose less and say some of the meanest things about yourself?

Why do you choose:

Bondage over Freedom?

Worrier over Warrior?

Fear over Confidence?

Temporary over Eternal?

Samuel K. Anderson (Whispers from My Mother)

Whispers from My Mother

DAY 203

Tremble!!!

Trembling trembles resembling

the fears assembled rambling ensembles.

Tremble!!! tremble!!! tremble!!!

Oh, ye old fears of mine.

Today is the day of your verdict of eviction.

Get all your ensembles and assemble

for your trembling verdict of eternal evacuated

destruction.

Samuel K. Anderson (Whispers from My Mother)

Whispers from My Mother

DAY 204

"So Loved"

How do you know you are "so loved" if you do not understand the term, word, energy, or the force of love? What's the epitomized definition of the term, word, energy, or force of love? That's the beginning to comprehending the intricacies of love and being "so loved".

Samuel K. Anderson (Whispers from My Mother)

Whispers from My Mother

DAY 205

Propensity

Propel your propensity
to prosper through proper
procedure in order to procure
proper perspective and progress
to attain versatile prosperity
lineage to posterity.

(Samuel K. Anderson (Whispers from My Mother)

… Whispers from My Mother

DAY 206

Heal

Heal and continue to heal
so high that you are able to
heal yourself from a higher
altitude and to heal others
when the need arises.

Samuel K. Anderson (Whispers from My Mother)

Whispers from My Mother

DAY 207

I Smile

I smile in my head all the time. Sometimes, I smile in my head so loud that my physical body has no option but to illuminate my inward smile outwardly for the entire universe to witness a glimpse of my inward eternal universe.

Samuel K. Anderson (Whispers from My Mother)

Whispers from My Mother

DAY 208

Slow Motion

Whenever you feel like things are moving so fast and you feel somewhat anxious, just pause everything; slow them down and watch them move in slow motion. After all, time is relative and diverse universe exist within you. The time of the flesh is neither the same as the time of the soul nor the infinite time of the spirit. Choose what universe you desire to live in and enjoy maneuvering through them.

Samuel K. Anderson (Whispers from My Mother)

Whispers from My Mother

DAY 209

Wasted

A day wasted is
a day failing to
unlearn to relearn.

Samuel K. Anderson (Whispers from My Mother)

DAY 210

Manifest

Admire great talents and gifts of others but never be jealous of them. Be inspired by them to aspire for your talents to be manifested.

Samuel K. Anderson (Whispers from My Mother)

Whispers from My Mother

Day 211

Maximization

Every human being can literally maximize anything they want or desire to maximize. Some of us fail because we tend to maximize the wrong things instead of the right ones. Maximization is at the front door of everyone. Just open your door to your world of unlimited maximization.

Samuel K. Anderson (Whispers from My Mother)

Whispers from My Mother

DAY 212

Pushups

When you fall down

in life, just try your

best to do some pushups

to activate your muscles

then bounce back in a

grand style to take what has

always been yours.

Samuel K. Anderson (Whispers from My Mother)

Whispers from My Mother

DAY 213

Emotions

He who is able to control his emotions can withstand almost any adversity by thinking and planning strategically through application of the philosophy of common sense.

Samuel K. Anderson (Whispers from My Mother)

Whispers from My Mother

DAY 214

Never Too Sunny

It's never too sunny

to step outside for

some vitamin D

from the sunny sun

especially if you have

some melanin in you.

Recharge that powerhouse

energy receptor in your DNA.

Samuel K. Anderson (Whispers from My Mother)

Whispers from My Mother

DAY 215

Recap

Before you sleep tonight

try to quickly recap your day;

no matter the conclusive outcome

just smile and tell yourself,

"this is just the beginning".

Samuel K. Anderson (Whispers from My Mother)

DAY 216

Perspective

It's not that they don't like you;

they are just not on your level.

You are one heck of a force

to reckon with; your company

is rare and not for everyone.

Samuel K. Anderson (Whispers from My Mother)

DAY 217

Madly Committed

In the midst of all

the chaos, bickering

and backbiting in the world;

be madly committed

to enjoying your own vibe in life.

Samuel K. Anderson (Whispers from My Mother)

DAY 218

The Fuel

Believe, believe,

believe, believe!!!

For that's the fuel

to drive your actions

to its destination.

Samuel K. Anderson (Whispers from My Mother)

Whispers from My Mother

DAY 219

Tell Yourself

Tell yourself about yourself
to your good self and allow
your good self to tell yourself
to become your better self.

Samuel K. Anderson (Whispers from My Mother)

DAY 220

Real

Life technically becomes

boring without

ups and downs.

Samuel K. Anderson (Whispers from My Mother)

Whispers from My Mother

DAY 221

No Amount of Money

Be persuasively convinced

in your commitment to pursue

your purpose to the extent

that no amount of money can

distract you from getting it done.

Samuel K. Anderson (Whispers from My Mother)

Whispers from My Mother

DAY 222

Every Day

Every day, you have
one hundred percent option
to choose either life or death.
Some choices illuminate
lifelong blessings while others
trigger lifelong curses.
Every single day is a terrific
opportunity to exercise such
freedom of life or death.

Samuel K. Anderson (Whispers from My Mother)

Whispers from My Mother

DAY 223

Thank You

One of the most powerful words that are of lightweight to say but of heavyweight in terms of positive energy and glory are the words of "thank you", yes; thank you.

Samuel K. Anderson (Whispers from My Mother)

Whispers from My Mother

DAY 224

Discovered

To be discovered by the world and the people in it, you need to be discovered by yourself. There is no grand discovery without self-discovery.

Samuel K. Anderson (Whispers from My Mother)

Whispers from My Mother

DAY 225

That's It

Every day should present

different motivation.

Every day will require different

thought process.

Every day meaning every single day,

but every day is not same day.

Samuel K. Anderson (Whispers from My Mother)

Whispers from My Mother

DAY 226

Misplaced

If you can buy all the fanciest clothes,

cars, houses and other material things

yet struggle to buy books upon books upon books

then you may be misplacing some of your priorities.

Samuel K. Anderson (Whispers from My Mother)

Whispers from My Mother

DAY 227

Careful Thoughts

In this journey, make sure

you surround yourself with those

that support you and that include your haters.

Your haters are some of the most brutally honest supporters you

need to have around you, not close to you.

Trust me, they are there to pump you up;

they themselves don't even know about that yet.

Samuel K. Anderson (Whispers from My Mother)

Whispers from My Mother

DAY 228

Mystery

One of the many mysteries
of death is that most people
do not know what lies behind it.
If everyone did then most people
may choose to exit this life
restricted in this physical body faster than
the rate at which we breathe.

Samuel K. Anderson (Whispers from My Mother)

Whispers from My Mother

DAY 229

In Grace

Be gracefully graceful
in your expressions of
your daily grace in full
gracefulness taking nothing
out of grace and everything in grace.

(Samuel K. Anderson (Whispers from My Mother)

Whispers from My Mother

DAY 230

Your Own Brain

Read as many books as possible.
There is nothing wrong to use those
books that interest you to "practice"
thought processing and decision making.
However, when it's time to "make" a decision
or "take" an action; you ought to use your own brain
and heart to decide what's best for you.
Such decisions are based on your culture,
traditions and laws that are unique from other cultures.
I encourage you to make decisions based on who you are, your
roots, your culture and your environment.

Samuel K. Anderson (Whispers from My Mother)

Whispers from My Mother

DAY 231

Distinction

A woman of grace,

elegance and wisdom

is a rare kind of distinction

calmly waiting within every woman

ready to be woken.

Samuel K. Anderson (Whispers from My Mother)

Whispers from My Mother

DAY 232

In Most Cases

It is physically discouraging to put in massive work yet tend to see little to no result. In most cases, that's because the bigger results are going through the germination phase underneath. Keep on putting in the work, adjust your mood and mindset.

Samuel K. Anderson (Whispers from My Mother)

Whispers from My Mother

DAY 233

Your Own

You have to listen

to your own because

it's only your own that

will write or narrate

true truth about your own.

Samuel K. Anderson (Whispers from My Mother)

Whispers from My Mother

DAY 234

Soulmate?

Are you my soulmate?

If so,

then be my *mate* to my *soul*,

my soulmate.

Eye to eye.

Mind to mind.

Heart to heart.

Soul to soul.

My mate, my soul,

my soulmate.

Samuel K. Anderson (Whispers from My Mother)

DAY 235

Dig Deep

Daily welcoming fears in your life

to cripple you from pursuing your aspirations

is just like purposefully welcoming

daily nightmares in your dreams.

Samuel K. Anderson (Whispers from My Mother)

Whispers from My Mother

DAY 236

Power

The brain has no limitations;
it can create all the unrealistic
realistic realities.
Physical manifestation of the brain's
creations are accomplished through
work, action, perseverance and discipline.

Samuel K. Anderson (Whispers from My Mother)

Whispers from My Mother

DAY 237

Access it

There's no human being without common sense; however, close to infinitesimal access this precious wealth of wisdom.

Samuel K. Anderson (Whispers from My Mother)

Whispers from My Mother

DAY 238

Reason

The reason why perfection is never achieved is because we never understood the concept of love until we exit this physical dimensional realm.

Samuel K. Anderson (Whispers from My Mother)

Whispers from My Mother

DAY 239

The Entities

There are different entities living within the man in the mirror.

Dreamers live in *Dreamland*.

Action takers live in *Actionland*.

Doers live in *DoerLand*.

Fear lives in *Fearland*.

Success lives in *Successland*.

Beasts live in *Beastland*.

Love lives in *Loveland*.

Wisdom lives in *Wisdomland*.

Determination lives in *Determinationland*.

All these entities can travel through and live at various lands with the sole permission by the man in the mirror.

Samuel K. Anderson (*Whispers from My Mother*)

# Whispers from My Mother

DAY 240

"Never"

Never is never

ever a perfect

reality of the whole truth.

Samuel K. Anderson (Whispers from My Mother)

Whispers from My Mother

DAY 241

P by G

People Healing Intentionally Love Independent Peace Propelled In Newly Esteemed Self

by

Gradually Harnessing All New Awareness.

Samuel K. Anderson (Whispers from My Mother)

Whispers from My Mother

DAY 242

Power of Prosperity

Prolific prologue of purposeful prosperity propagated by proliferation propensity intended to prolifically prolong its profound power of prosperity.

Samuel K. Anderson (Whispers from My Mother)

Whispers from My Mother

DAY 243

Permission

A determined mind
and heart is almost always
unstoppable without
the intended permission
of the individual in action.

Samuel K. Anderson (Whispers from My Mother)

Whispers from My Mother

DAY 244

Humility or Ego

One of the most difficult lessons to learn in life is the art of humility, as it requires you to lower your ego and exposes your vulnerabilities; yet, it's one of the utmost rewarding attributes needed to excel at almost everything in life.

Samuel K. Anderson (Whispers from My Mother)

Whispers from My Mother

DAY 245

Be Cautious

It's dangerous to be in a romantic relationship with someone who doesn't believe in you or what you stand for than to be in such relationship with a known enemy.

Samuel K. Anderson (Whispers from My Mother)

Whispers from My Mother

DAY 246

Games We Play

We all seem to play games on each other

in almost always every situation.

Some games are mild and unintended to cause

hurt, pain or vengeance while some are the opposite

to the aforementioned.

Yet, most of us claim ignorance of our contributions

when the outcome is inversely proportional

to our projected outcome.

Samuel K. Anderson (Whispers from My Mother)

Whispers from My Mother

DAY 247

if

If is such a simple word

yet holds so much power in both

an unimaginable and imaginable

way.

If one will succeed or not succeed

is based on how one defines the word

"*if*".

Is your definition of "*if*" holding you back

or is it pushing you to become the person that

you were born to be, which is someone with a purpose.

Samuel K. Anderson (Whispers from My Mother)

Whispers from My Mother

DAY 248

Address

Words can undress you

and it's not only sapiosexuals,

but the same words can address you

and dress you with a covering

of dignity and respect.

Samuel K. Anderson (Whispers from My Mother)

Whispers from My Mother

DAY 249

Be It

Hear it.

Feel it.

Embrace it.

Love it.

Move with it.

Wear it.

Understand it.

Grow and learn it.

Succeed with it.

Never reject it.

Be it.

That's you.

You are a spirit.

Got it?

Now, live it.

Samuel K. Anderson (Whispers from My Mother)

Whispers from My Mother

DAY 250

Those Moments

There are times that we all

seem to lack the needed inspiration

to keep on keeping on; that extra boast

to get us a step closer to our goal.

That moment when you get caught off guard, pressed with time

and running out of gas.

It's almost like feeling utterly exhausted and sleepy at midnight but

your final paper is due early morning.

At times like that, we all need to;

refresh our minds,

evaluate the task at hand and

decide to dedicate to get it done.

Samuel K. Anderson (Whispers from My Mother)

Whispers from My Mother

DAY 251

The Future is Present

Do something today
that will change the life
of numerous generations yet
to be born. Believe it or not,
an unborn generation would be
affected by your present contributions.

Samuel K. Anderson (Whispers from My Mother)

Whispers from My Mother

DAY 252

Neutrality of Consistency

Consistency is a neutral energy
that works for you depending on
the state of your energy input.
If you put in hard work backed by
consistency, the eventual outcome is a successful one.
If you put in a "consistent" lazy energy
you are definitely going to reap zero productivity. That's the
neutrality of consistency.

Samuel K. Anderson (Whispers from My Mother)

Whispers from My Mother

DAY 253

The Phrase

I used to struggle to accept

the phrase, " there's time for everything"

until I learned that

patience, knowledge, hope and wisdom

are necessary to understand the concept

of time and my role in it all.

Samuel K. Anderson (Whispers from My Mother)

Whispers from My Mother

DAY 254

Today's Tomorrow

If tomorrow never comes,

then today never ends.

Tomorrow's plans are plans of hope,

belief and the faith of a better encounter

greater than today.

Samuel K. Anderson (Whispers from My Mother)

Whispers from My Mother

DAY 255

Decentralization of Centralization

Centralization of modern societies has made us think that the world is almost overpopulated. One of the many solutions at least for now is decentralization and reallocation of resources and institutions to abandoned villages, towns and unused lands factoring wildlife and agriculture into the planning for a better development of present generation and posterity.

Samuel K. Anderson (Whispers from My Mother)

Whispers from My Mother

DAY 256

What's Fear or Favor

Fear or favor may only take you so far

in this life on planet earth

but your effort in putting in the work is needed

to live a life free of fear and uncertainties.

Samuel K. Anderson (Whispers from My Mother)

Whispers from My Mother

DAY 257

Wisdom Sets Us Free

We are all controlled to some extent in pursuit of institutionalized knowledge; regardless of our religious affiliations, country of origin or residence. However, wisdom sets us free from the helms of societal control and oppression.

Samuel K. Anderson (Whispers from My Mother)

DAY 258

Wavelengths of Words

We sometimes fall.

We rise.

We stand tall.

We wiggle in low confidence

or we push through confidence

and all these things happen because of words.

Words are powerful wavelengths of immeasurable energy.

Samuel K. Anderson (Whispers from My Mother)

Whispers from My Mother

DAY 259

Its Wholeness

One of the unique things about this life is that, whether you accept your purpose in life or consciously/unconsciously deny yourself of any chance to become "*who*" or "*what*" you were meant to be; we will all go through life's journey no matter your stance in life. The question then is, what kind of journey are you embarking? Confusion, frustration, excuses, blaming, difficulties, unfairness, and deceit are not exceptions to the journey rather part of its wholeness.

Samuel K. Anderson (Whispers from My Mother)

Whispers from My Mother

DAY 260

Equality and Equity

Equality and equity are not the same words, but both are equally important and effective when used without appropriating justification to be synonymous.

Samuel K. Anderson (Whispers from My Mother)

Whispers from My Mother

DAY 261

is it

What is priceless peace of mind

to a financially rich person

with no joy, good health or happiness.

Samuel K. Anderson (Whispers from My Mother)

Whispers from My Mother

DAY 262

Succinctly

Be succinct in your ways

to strategically think through things

in order to succinctly communicate

through actions with integrity, accountability

and probity.

Samuel K. Anderson (Whispers from My Mother)

Whispers from My Mother

DAY 263

The "Hope"

Every human being has hope

consciousness or unconsciously.

There is no life without hope.

So long as you are breathing,

you are hopeful.

In that, to have life is to have hope

and to have hope is to have life.

It doesn't end at the end of this physical life.

Be hopeful with your hope and hopefully

you will embrace hope while your heart

keeps on pumping.

Samuel K. Anderson (Whispers from My Mother)

Whispers from My Mother

DAY 264

Faith & Spirituality

If we are all spiritual beings in a physical form,

then what stops us from living and continuously encountering

spiritual manifestations and transformations in physical reality?

It is simply because most of us have little to no faith.

We are doubters by default automation. Most of us even doubt

before they can grant themselves the opportunity to believe.

Faith is essential for spirituality.

Samuel K. Anderson (Whispers from My Mother)

Whispers from My Mother

DAY 265

Be Diligent

Be confident in your ways

and never be ashamed

or apologize for your confidence;

however, be diligent to admit when you

know that you are wrong.

Samuel K. Anderson (Whispers from My Mother)

Whispers from My Mother

DAY 266

Little Liliate

Little Liliate was the littlest of all the little lads.

The little lads' littleness had little impact on their little leagues until little Liliate, the littlest lights up with her little skills to win it all at the little lads' league.

Samuel K. Anderson (Whispers from My Mother)

DAY 267

Explored Mind

A mind willing to explore

is a mind capable to be free.

Samuel K. Anderson (Whispers from My Mother)

Whispers from My Mother

DAY 268

Be! Be!! Be!!!

To say it cannot be done

is an automatic defeat in itself

and to have a doubt before pursuing a goal

is fifty percent failure of progress.

Samuel K. Anderson (Whispers from My Mother)

Whispers from My Mother

DAY 269

Heart & Mind

My heart has many thoughts

and many thoughts come to my mind

but at the end of the day; it's my mind

that determines what thoughts stays

and what thoughts are thrown out

through the windows of my heart.

Samuel K. Anderson (Whispers from My Mother)

Whispers from My Mother

DAY 270

You Are

Why do you try so hard

to not become what others say

or think you are instead of becoming

who you believe you are.

Samuel K. Anderson (Whispers from My Mother)

Whispers from My Mother

DAY 271

The Good in Everything

What's the good in good morning, good afternoon or good night if the morning, afternoon or night wasn't so good?

Well, the good in the morning, afternoon or night is the light of your life that shines continuously while you read these words.

The very vibrations of your soul and spirit synchronizing to propel light and life in you every day.

Yes, that's the good in everything.

Samuel K. Anderson (Whispers from My Mother)

Whispers from My Mother

DAY 272

Best Way

Don't be afraid to face

your worse self

because

that's the best way to correct it.

Samuel K. Anderson (Whispers from My Mother)

Whispers from My Mother

DAY 273

Love-Faith-Hope

Hope, the belief of a better tomorrow.

Faith, the audacity to work today towards a better tomorrow.

Love, the fuel of life for our very existence.

They all need to be in full function for your life to steer in the right direction.

Samuel K. Anderson (Whispers from My Mother)

DAY 274

Discretionary Power

At your discretion as much as you are in control of your mind and spirit; you have the power to rebuke as many times as possible anything that your gut tells you that it doesn't belong to your life's purpose.

Samuel K. Anderson (Whispers from My Mother)

Whispers from My Mother

DAY 275

Best Place

The best place to see yourself
is at the solemn place
of meditation and fasting.

Samuel K. Anderson (Whispers from My Mother)

DAY 276

Respect Your Roots

You will never ever be complete

regardless of how wealthy or how poor

you are; so long as you reject who you are

with direct respect to your root, culture and traditions

while you value the very things you are not.

Samuel K. Anderson (Whispers from My Mother)

Whispers from My Mother

DAY 277

The word "DO"

How you _say_ things

and how you _perceive_ things

doesn't define you;

rather how you _do_ things and what you _do_

when in a position to decide good or bad

tells everything about you.

Samuel K. Anderson (Whispers from My Mother)

Whispers from My Mother

DAY 278

Unique

We all have our likes and dislikes,

our favorites and least favorites,

our strengths and weaknesses,

and that's what make us unique.

Hence, to know yourself is to

accept yourself,

to accept yourself is to value yourself,

to value yourself is to love yourself,

and to love yourself is to know who you are.

Samuel K. Anderson (Whispers from My Mother)

Whispers from My Mother

DAY 279

Push

Push yourself and give it
your all to pass your
psychologically personalized limits
and see how you'll surprise yourself
with new limits every day.

Samuel K. Anderson (Whispers from My Mother)

Whispers from My Mother

DAY 280

Unseen

Everything in creation living and non-living move through time, space, waves and sounds.

The fact that you cannot detect its movement doesn't defy its performance of movement.

What's important is for you to identify your rhythm within all the three heavens and on planet earth.

That's only when you may come close to all the movements happening through time, space, waves and sounds.

Samuel K. Anderson (Whispers from My Mother)

Whispers from My Mother

DAY 281

Flow of my Spirit and Consciousness

The flow of water reminds me of the flow of my spirit and consciousness.

Its power is hidden within its serenity.

Its flow of purpose is untamed regardless of the obstacles in its paths.

Its capabilities are endless as it changes from liquid to solid, from solid to vapor and from vapor back to its original form through condensation.

You will know that nothing is meant to break you when you know your consciousness and spirit. The body will automatically be in line when your soul and spirit is in uniform flow.

Samuel K. Anderson (Whispers from My Mother)

Whispers from My Mother

DAY 282

The Happenings

What is happening

are things that are supposed

to happen to pave way

for the good things that are meant

to happen to happen.

Samuel K. Anderson (Whispers from My Mother)

Whispers from My Mother

DAY 283

A World of Madness

We live in a world of madness whereby mad people do not even know that they're mad. Rather, they laugh at the very few that are sane thinking that they are rather the mad ones.

Samuel K. Anderson (Whispers from My Mother)

Whispers from My Mother

DAY 284

Don't Be a Fool

You can play one hundred percent stupid

with people and get away with it

but you can never play stupid with *God, The Creator.*

Samuel K. Anderson (Whispers from My Mother)

… Whispers from My Mother

DAY 285

Psyche

The easiest way to lose yourself

or to lose almost everything is to be afraid.

Fear is a disastrous epidemic

that can easily shut your entire

system down starting from your psyche.

Samuel K. Anderson (Whispers from My Mother)

Whispers from My Mother

DAY 286

Scare

What you don't know

cannot scare you.

What eventually scares you

are the things you think you know

and the things that doesn't kill you

within what you think you know;

only makes your energy stronger.

Samuel K. Anderson (Whispers from My Mother)

Whispers from My Mother

DAY 287

Tree of Knowledge

In eating from the tree of knowledge; we rather became spiritually ignorant and physically docile than intellectually knowledgeable. In that, death, sickness, old age, and all kinds of troubles are upon us. We have traded living in eternity on earth with the Creator's presence to just a distant life in a jiffy full of troubles.

Samuel K. Anderson (Whispers from My Mother)

Whispers from My Mother

DAY 288

This Time

God, The Creator never change.

It's only mankind that changes.

The Creator do exactly what He says

He will do. Mankind is disloyal,

dishonest, and full of ignorance.

Mankind fails to do what we commit

to do; which is to obey The Creator's

commandments and instructions.

What has been said by The Creator

will happen. Everything mankind has

experienced in the past, everything currently

experiencing, and all the experiences yet to happen

have all happened before but this time with fire.

Samuel K. Anderson (Whispers from My Mother)

Whispers from My Mother

DAY 289

The Birth

The birth of every child

is the birth of a new generation.

It remains our responsibility

to properly educate every new generation

that we are blessed with to be better

than previous generations for a better posterity.

Samuel K. Anderson (*Whispers from My Mother*)

Whispers from My Mother

DAY 290

Real Actions

No amount of talking,

fussing, anger, threats,

complaints, or arrogance

will ever solve an issue

if real actions are not taken

to resolve the dissolve.

Samuel K. Anderson (Whispers from My Mother)

Whispers from My Mother

DAY 291

Listening and Hearing

You can intimidate people to listen to you but you can never false them to hear you. There's a big difference between listening and hearing. The latter is keen.

Samuel K. Anderson (Whispers from My Mother)

Whispers from My Mother

DAY 292

Opportunities

We discredit many

opportunities than

granting opportunities

to all the opportunities that

come to us in our lifetime.

Samuel K. Anderson (Whispers from My Mother)

Whispers from My Mother

DAY 293

Can You See!!!

If only we could see our

complete supernatural abilities

as spiritual beings trapped in a flesh

then we will never be afraid of anything.

Samuel K. Anderson (*Whispers from My Mother*)

Whispers from My Mother

DAY 294

Take Time

Don't rush to eat your mangoes

when they're not ripe.

It's tough to not get frustrated

with all the no's in life.

Take time to work on yourself,

for when the time is right;

nothing can stop you from excelling.

Samuel K. Anderson (Whispers from My Mother)

Whispers from My Mother

DAY 295

1 on 1

Every relationship deserves honesty
no matter how small or big the situation may be.
Be true with your feelings to communicate
them with your partner;
especially, the most difficult or complicated ones.

Samuel K. Anderson (Whispers from My Mother)

Whispers from My Mother

DAY 296

Battles

The best battles
worth winning
in life are the ones
in our heads.

Samuel K. Anderson (Whispers from My Mother)

Whispers from My Mother

DAY 297

It Hurts

Put your body through the pain of hard work and don't stop your body from working when it hurts the most; for the night is portioned for the body's rest but the spirit is at work 24/7 while the soul rests with the body.

Samuel K. Anderson (Whispers from My Mother)

Whispers from My Mother

DAY 298

What Gives

Water is very essential

to life's sustainability

but the same water

can easily kill someone;

however, that doesn't reduce

the important quality of water.

Samuel K. Anderson (Whispers from My Mother)

Whispers from My Mother

DAY 299

Rare

Love yourself.

Keep yourself private from people.

It's best to make them wonder about you

than to know almost everything about you.

Remember, you are not a public newspaper.

You are a rare kind and you need to stay

that way to be mysterious.

Samuel K. Anderson (Whispers from My Mother)

DAY 300

Move On

You made a mistake.

Acknowledge it.

Be accountable and learn from it.

Now, move on to life's next mystery

of growth, love, and more learning.

Samuel K. Anderson (Whispers from My Mother)

Whispers from My Mother

DAY 301

The World

We all see the world differently

and it mostly depends on the way

we were brought up

and what we were exposed to;

never allow that to cripple you

from becoming the best version of yourself

no matter your upbringing.

Samuel K. Anderson (Whispers from My Mother)

Whispers from My Mother

DAY 302

Deprive Me Not

We have been deceived to chase things

that cost us an arm and leg

making us lifeless and heartless

while depriving ourselves from things

that are free and priceless like laughter,

happiness, joy, appreciation, good rest, and self-love.

Samuel K. Anderson (Whispers from My Mother)

Whispers from My Mother

DAY 303

Shift

If we can get the whole world to meditate for at least thirty minutes a day with zero distractions only then can we see a gradual shift towards the fullness in our oneness as a people globally.

Samuel K. Anderson (Whispers from My Mother)

Whispers from My Mother

DAY 304

Leadership & Time

A true leader must lead without fear or favor yet willing to adapt to the ever-changing times in order to stay current on issues and to develop tangible strategies capable of producing realistic results.

Samuel K. Anderson (Whispers from My Mother)

Whispers from My Mother

DAY 305

Psychological Deficiencies

One of the tests you will face is seeing the ones you love uninterested in seeking knowledge or wisdom and being destroyed in their complacency yet unbothered to even try to free themselves from their psychological deficiencies in most cases until it's too late.

Samuel K. Anderson (Whispers from My Mother)

Whispers from My Mother

DAY 306

Some of Us

How does it feel to help someone to get to a better spot in life; yet, you see yourself struggling with no one to motivate you in person when you also need it. We all need a little push from time to time but some of us just have to push ourselves at all times to get to the next level.

Samuel K. Anderson (Whispers from My Mother)

Whispers from My Mother

DAY 307

Recurring

Pay attention to those who are never appreciative. They don't deserve your time and energy.

Samuel K. Anderson (Whispers from My Mother)

Whispers from My Mother

DAY 308

Fighter

You have to fight.

Fight very hard

and be willing to fight every day

in this physical dimension called life.

Samuel K. Anderson (*Whispers from My Mother*)

Whispers from My Mother

DAY 309

Make it happen.

Be able to think.

Think a lot.

The good, bad, ugly and in between.

Think it through.

Think about it all.

Think about the best and worthwhile thoughts within your thoughts.

Then, be ready to go very hard and all out on execution.

Make it happen.

Samuel K. Anderson (Whispers from My Mother)

Whispers from My Mother

DAY 310

Those Moments

Pitch black, blocked, dead end and no way out.

Helpless, weak, underappreciated and frustrated.

If you haven't felt this or journeyed through this before, then you have not fully been tested in life.

Some give in.

Others hold on for a while.

While, very few make it out.

Where are you in life? What is your journey?

What are you going to do about your journey?

You are accountable for whatever you decide.

Samuel K. Anderson (Whispers from My Mother)

Whispers from My Mother

DAY 311

Desired

Do you just love

the thought of me,

the presence of me,

the existence of me,

the beauty of me with or without makeup,

the strengths I exhibit,

or

the fullness of me with all my imperfections yet to be known to you.

Because,

I am more than what you think of me.

I am a spiritual being,

I am a conscious soul,

within this flesh that drew your attention.

Samuel K. Anderson (Whispers from My Mother)

Whispers from My Mother

DAY 312

Benjamins & Fools

Money can easily make you a fool.

It can easily change you for the worst

inhumane version of yourself.

Money is a test of one's true personality.

Money doesn't make you, rather you make money.

The solution is to be willing to lose the money at the expense of

losing yourself to it.

A fool with money doesn't profit the community.

Money is not just physical but more of a spiritual entity. It's a

"granted energy" to carry the transactions of specific generations.

Money is more than what you think it is. Many do not understand

money and may never come close to comprehend it.

Samuel K. Anderson (Whispers from My Mother)

Whispers from My Mother

DAY 313

Freeing Your Mindset

It's a challenge to change a mind that has been heavily indoctrinated with hundreds of years of lies believing that he or she is not capable of leading, achieving massive successes and walking in greatness. It's a great challenge but it can definitely be done.

Samuel K. Anderson (Whispers from My Mother)

Whispers from My Mother

DAY 314

Disciplined Lesson

There are going to be times that you may make some mistakes as a leader, a teacher, a motivator or a legacy setter. When confronted by these mistakes, don't allow your ego of achievements deprive you from humbly acknowledging and learning from your mishaps. This could be one of the simplest yet toughest lessons of discipline to you.

Samuel K. Anderson (Whispers from My Mother)

Whispers from My Mother

DAY 315

Thy Parents

Never in your life
be ashamed of your parents
no matter their economic or
social status to impress
your current status.

Samuel K. Anderson (Whispers from My Mother)

Whispers from My Mother

DAY 316

Your Truths

Be confident in your discoveries

of your truths and walk in grace;

never ashamed of any of them

for they are your strength to catapult

you to self-appreciation, self-love and growth.

Samuel K. Anderson (Whispers from My Mother)

Whispers from My Mother

DAY 317

What's Worth

Good psychological
and physical health
are richer and worthwhile
than billions of gold.

Samuel K. Anderson (Whispers from My Mother)

Whispers from My Mother

DAY 318

Right Thing

Sometimes, I go to feed the birds
on the streets and in my neighborhood.
It's not because the birds may die of hunger
or may not find their own food.
It's because it's the right thing to execute.

Samuel K. Anderson (Whispers from My Mother)

Whispers from My Mother

DAY 319

Warrants

It's best to tell the truth and stand with the truth at all times than to lie for a brief escape from a situation. Nothing goes unchecked within the universe. Everything is either rewarded or punished. To lie is to set your consciousness on death warrants; hence, the more you lie the more slaughter you assign to your consciousness.

Samuel K. Anderson (Whispers from My Mother)

Whispers from My Mother

DAY 320

How Dare You

You did not give life to yourself
to enter into this physical realm,
so how dare you take the life given
to you; to waste it on death instead of
life full of experiences regardless
of its challenges.

Samuel K. Anderson (Whispers from My Mother)

Whispers from My Mother

DAY 321

Immortality

We are all immortal though not in the flesh yet in the spirit we are as immortal as the image of *The Creator*.

Death can only hold the flesh for a moment passage of its last breathes as the spirit exits the flesh to its immortal life in eternity; just like vapor exits a hot surface.

Samuel K. Anderson (Whispers from My Mother)

Whispers from My Mother

DAY 322

The Focus

Do not focus on
the feelings of
the word; rather
focus on the truths
of the word.

Samuel K. Anderson (Whispers from My Mother)

Whispers from My Mother

DAY 323

Say It

You cannot expect

to live an unrighteous life

and be righteously rewarded.

It will never happen.

Samuel K. Anderson (Whispers from My Mother)

Whispers from My Mother

DAY 324

Hope for You

My hope for you all young and future generations is to love wisdom and nurture. You will be joyful in your ways and hopeful in your life. Success and grace will be with you and laughter will be your perfume.

Samuel K. Anderson (Whispers from My Mother)

Whispers from My Mother

DAY 325

Virtuous

It is better to live

a short life full of virtues

than a long life full

of wickedness and destruction.

Samuel K. Anderson (Whispers from My Mother)

DAY 326

"Ka"

Our own wickedness

becomes

our own punishment.

Samuel K. Anderson (Whispers from My Mother)

Whispers from My Mother

DAY 327

Best Parts of a Woman

A woman's character, mind and heart

are her best parts but above

all else is her sophisticated spirit.

A wise man is the man that sees

these things in a woman instead of her

physical physique which is just as temporary

as a breath leaving your nostrils.

Samuel K. Anderson (Whispers from My Mother)

Whispers from My Mother

DAY 328

The Gray

I may not have gray hair yet

but

my words are grayed.

Samuel K. Anderson (Whispers from My Mother)

Whispers from My Mother

DAY 329

Purpose Fulfilled

Service to others is a blessing of a purpose fulfilled.

There is no success without an intent to serve consciously or unconsciously. Service leads success and without service there would be complete chaos and disorder in the entire universe.

Everything is defined in the art of service.

Purpose denied is service denied.

Samuel K. Anderson (Whispers from My Mother)

Whispers from My Mother

DAY 330

Doors

There are many doors in our lives that can open at any time with the right energy, attitude and communication.

There is the door of faith, service, prayer, wisdom, wealth, good health, influence, grace, fulfilment and appreciation.

These doors are fresh every day; make sure to use as many as possible every day.

Samuel K. Anderson (Whispers from My Mother)

Whispers from My Mother

DAY 331

Distinctive Distinction

Do not be intimidated by another person's wealth, greatness and influence.

You have equally important and effective treasures of greatness in you.

Tap into it and be your own kind of person of valor.

Samuel K. Anderson (Whispers from My Mother)

Whispers from My Mother

DAY 332

Ignorance

Ignorance of the truth doesn't make it a lie; rather, it puts you at a psychological disadvantage.

Samuel K. Anderson (Whispers from My Mother)

Whispers from My Mother

DAY 333

Wise Counsel

The thoughts of a person
without the guidance of wisdom
is corrupt and yield results planted
in greed, selfishness and destruction.
The counsel of every wise person is found
only in *The Most High*.

Samuel K. Anderson (*Whispers from My Mother*)

Whispers from My Mother

DAY 334

Success Triggers

Your abilities married with consistent optimism will land you the success you desire. The road on which you travel to get to your personalized self-actualization is called attitude. Your route of attitude will test you and will either fail you or catapult you.

Pay attention on the road of attitude.

Samuel K. Anderson (Whispers from My Mother)

Whispers from My Mother

DAY 335

Mood, Mind & Power

At this very moment, what's going on in your mind? Are you analyzing all the problems in your life with your family, friends, career, and the universe to the point that you are literally lost in your own existence?

Right this moment, this very micro-second that just passed; what have you been thinking of? Are you feeling like you hit rock bottom and all hope is lost? Are you in a panic mode? Feeling anxious and overwhelm at the same time? The good news is that, you and I control everything that goes through our mind. You and I can pick and choose what we want to analyze through our mind. You and I have the audacity as human beings to request, require, demand and prophesy into our *now* and our *future*. So, cheer up and make the best outcome of your current situation come true.

Samuel K. Anderson (Whispers from My Mother)

Whispers from My Mother

DAY 336

Feeling Jealous?

Sometimes in your romantic relationship,

you may feel jealous from time to time.

Jealousy in a romantic relationship is not a bad thing.

It's natural to feel jealous,

this is because you love the person you are in a relationship with.

Do not allow the feeling of jealousy to emotionally control you.

Rather, communicate clearly with your partner

by letting your partner know how you feel about some behaviors.

Naturally, we tend to be jealous when we extremely

care or love someone.

Make sure it doesn't consume you,

because; the entire romantic relationship can go into flames.

Samuel K. Anderson (Whispers from My Mother)

Whispers from My Mother

DAY 337

Good Friends are very Rare

Depending on friends to feel loved and as a means of approval is a treacherous road to take. Do not forget that good friends are very rare. Most of them are your friends because you have something to offer. When you get into a tough situation and happen to lose everything you had, unable to give to the friends you thought were there for you; you wouldn't find them. The real ones are super rare because mankind is simply selfish and greedy. Remember, we all came into this world individually. You were brought here by a divine power; you need to be in connection with that divine power. Pray every day, love yourself first, take very good care of your health and always be the best friend you ever had to yourself. When it's all said and done, we depart this earth alone just like the way we arrived. This is not separatism rather a reality within your very existence.

Samuel K. Anderson (Whispers from My Mother)

Whispers from My Mother

DAY 338

Living in Reverse

Could our world be living life in reverse mode?

Instead of training children in mostly theory, could we push for early vocational skills? Hands on experiences whereby children, teens and young adults at an early stage of their lives are capable of discovering their gifts or talents instead of just grades?

Could all the thoughts of getting out of earth be a reverse life instead of fixing what we have destroyed on earth and taking care of things; since this is the only possible place for humans?

Could wars, hate, racism, divisions, greed, and terror be the main reason why civilization keeps on slowing, retrogressing and dumbing down instead of progression, unity, strength and a better earth. Could we all meditate on these rhetoric realities to find a possible solution for mankind's wellbeing?

Samuel K. Anderson (Whispers from My Mother)

Whispers from My Mother

DAY 339

Don't Rob Yourself

Don't rob yourself of the daily opportunities
to learn from both the little things and the big ones too.
Every word, phrase, sentence, paragraph,
chapter, article, book, conversations,
and all the daily activities present tremendous
opportunities for you to learn, grow
and become better than yesterday.

Samuel K. Anderson (Whispers from My Mother)

Whispers from My Mother

DAY 340

Reverence

Our life on earth is as relatively short as food entering and exiting the alimentary canal. Why do you boast of things that you don't rightfully own? You came into this world naked and you will surely exit the same way.

As a reminder, just take a look at yourself whenever you shower or bath. We all enter the shower or bath tab naked and exit out of it naked. This is another daily reminder to remain humble and fearful in reverence of *The Most High Goa.*

Samuel K. Anderson (*Whispers from My Mother*)

Whispers from My Mother

DAY 341

a Video

A video is worth all its recorded time. It may be the only evidence to prove your innocence especially if you are at the disadvantaged end of the law.

Samuel K. Anderson (Whispers from My Mother)

Whispers from My Mother

DAY 342

Untouchable

The art of acquiring new *knowledge*
and *knowing* is sweet for those that seek it,
but have you encountered wisdom?
Wisdom is at an untouchable level.

Samuel K. Anderson (Whispers from My Mother)

Whispers from My Mother

DAY 343

Multilateralism

Multilateralism will never work
unless "*racism*" is retired and made illegal.
I wonder why so-called professional businesses,
companies, governments and top universities
still enforce "*race categorization*"
when it is very well known that "*race*" is a huge fallacy,
unprovable and one hundred percent unscientific.

Samuel K. Anderson (Whispers from My Mother)

Whispers from My Mother

DAY 344

Integrity

Integrity is the tool

needed

for versatility that reflects

one's longevity.

Samuel K. Anderson (Whispers from My Mother)

Whispers from My Mother

DAY 345

The Cause

If you build your empire

on foundations of lies, greed,

and fear; this empire will never last.

The same lies, greed and fear

will be the cause of your empire's collapse.

Samuel K. Anderson (Whispers from My Mother)

Whispers from My Mother

DAY 346

Important Core

As the man of the household, your leadership

is more important than the amount of money

you make for the family.

The wife and children see your exemplary leadership

and through that, the pace and outcome of the family are set.

A man is a man for a reason

and a woman is a woman for a reason too.

Do not lose focus of this important core instituted by *The Creator.*

Samuel K. Anderson (*Whispers from My Mother*)

Whispers from My Mother

DAY 347

Humility

Humility is a vital strength;

very few discover its power

due to

blindness of pride.

Samuel K. Anderson (Whispers from My Mother)

Whispers from My Mother

DAY 348

It's okay to cry

It's okay to cry as a man.

Yes, it is normal to cry as a man.

In fact, it is natural to cry as a man.

You are made up of about seventy percent water.

Let it flow.

Clean that dirt that stained your spirit and soul.

Those tears don't make you less of a man;

it rather makes you a real man, which is scarce these days.

Samuel K. Anderson (Whispers from My Mother)

Whispers from My Mother

DAY 349

A World Full of...

In a world full of hate, war, bigotry,

deception, greed, selfishness, destruction,

lies, "fakeness", and restlessness;

try your best to always live with a strong mind

that is true to your virtues and consistent with your actions.

Samuel K. Anderson (Whispers from My Mother)

Whispers from My Mother

DAY 350

Unaware vs Aware

When you are unaware, miseducated, or inexperienced; people may tend to take advantage of your ignorance and may hurt you emotionally, psychologically or monetarily.

When you are aware, properly educated, knowledgeable and current with informational updates; you ought to be vigilant in your actions or you may take advantage of your own self. Do no act based on emotions, anger or pride. Move, act, and make decisions strategically through wise counselling to achieve greater goals beneficial to your mission, vision, integrity, family and community.

Samuel K. Anderson (Whispers from My Mother)

Whispers from My Mother

DAY 351

Too Consumed

Make sure you make time for the people

who check up on you.

These are the few people in your life

that care about your health and overall wellbeing.

Don't be too consumed in life to fail to acknowledge

these precious jewels that come once in a lifetime.

Samuel K. Anderson (Whispers from My Mother)

Whispers from My Mother

DAY 352

Don't be Bitter

Don't be bitter towards those that you once helped who turned out to be ungrateful and disrespectful.

Samuel K. Anderson (Whispers from My Mother)

Whispers from My Mother

DAY 353

No Exception

There's something called life. No living person can cheat it. It will handle you with no mercy if you keep on screwing up. It has its own moments of punishments and rewards. Happy is the one who gains its blessings.

Learn to be good to it.

Be true to it.

Appreciate it.

Enjoy it.

Use it as a service to others.

Learn from it.

Grow with and within it.

This is something that all living things must go through with no exception.

Samuel K. Anderson (Whispers from My Mother)

Whispers from My Mother

DAY 354

A Walking Billionaire

Each individual in the world is at least a million-dollar business entity. Some are worth trillions and billions in business ownership without knowing, simply because about ninety nine percent of the world populace lack faith. We are all providing services to each other in one way or another. Viewing things through the business spectacles, one percent of eight billion population is around eighty million people worldwide. This means, over seven billion nine hundred twenty million people are just walking around failing to achieve their purpose.

Start that business you have been hesitant to begin because the world needs your full services, gifts, mindset and inspiration.

Samuel K. Anderson (Whispers from My Mother)

Whispers from My Mother

DAY 355

Receive

Let go of all evil thoughts and evil eyes;

embrace your daily blessings of wealth, health and wisdom.

Free yourself from all negativities and let positive energy

flow through you like a spring of eternal water.

Samuel K. Anderson (Whispers from My Mother)

Whispers from My Mother

DAY 356 - Now, is The Time

Be true to your core.

The tune to the culture doesn't change.

It is who you are, your roots.

Why are you confused?

Why are you begging?

Don't you know you are the chosen?

The magnet of your strength is in unity.

So, why do you hate thy brother?

Why do you reject your own?

Now, you see why you are powerless?

Come back to your senses.

Stand for what you believe.

Do not ever be afraid of another man.

You must stop wandering.

Turn on the music to the tune of your consciousness.

Arise, unite immediately and fight together as one.

Now, is the time. Unite, unite, unite!
Samuel K. Anderson (Whispers from My Mother)

Whispers from My Mother

DAY 357 - The Truth You Seek

You pray for it.

You scream for it.

You cry for it.

You want it.

You demand it.

You call for it.

Would you even know, if I expose it to you?

Can you accept it regardless of how it makes you feel?

Would you turn away from your foolishness if it requires you to?

Would you give up your numbness for your awareness?

Would it wake you up from your psychological comma?

Look around you, tell me what you see.

The truth you seek has been within you since birth.

You rejected it either consciously or unconsciously

when you came face to face with it.

Did you notice it? Because, I just exposed it to you.

The truth you seek.
Samuel K. Anderson (Whispers from My Mother)

Whispers from My Mother

DAY 358

Why and What

What you do may
not necessarily
be *why* you do it.
If *why* you do it
is your core purpose
then *what* you do
should be *what* you do
regardless of
what people think of you.
Your *why* is your reason.
Your *what* is your output.
Your *what* without your *why*
is vain, deadly, and meaningless.
Your *why* with your *what*
is your utmost liberation
that needs no external approval.
Samuel K. Anderson (Whispers from My Mother)

Whispers from My Mother

DAY 359

Reason Why You are Powerless

One of the main reasons

why you are powerless

and may remain powerless forever

is because you either don't know

who your real enemies are

or you are too delusional to know

that you are desperately and

pathetically begging your enemies

to torture you.

Samuel K. Anderson (Whispers from My Mother)

Whispers from My Mother

DAY 360

Difference Between You and I

The difference between you and I

is that you think you know me

but I know very well that I know myself.

Hence, the reason why I move the way I move.

I talk the way I talk.

I walk the way I walk.

I speak the way I speak.

Thinking you know me is where you fell off;

because I really don't care about what you think.

Knowing myself is key to my being.

Samuel K. Anderson (Whispers from My Mother)

Whispers from My Mother

DAY 361

Move in Silence

Be calm.

Be gentle.

Don't be rattled by all the loud noise.

Move in silence.

Emerge in your greatness.

Power can be expressed in excellence and grace.

In most cases,

the powerful movers and shakers

are behind the scenes until it's

necessary to take center stage.

Samuel K. Anderson (Whispers from My Mother)

Whispers from My Mother

DAY 362 - The Heart

The heart is very precious,

the first beat is the life it gives;

to love,

to heal,

to promise,

to protect,

to unite,

to serve,

to touch other lives,

to keep on beating for life,

to hate,

to kill,

to destroy,

to deceive,

and to separate.

The last beat of it is the last goodbye.

Take very good care of your heart.

Samuel K. Anderson (Whispers from My Mother)

Whispers from My Mother

DAY 363

"Never Give Up"

I refuse to give up.

Why should I?

I can't find any valid reason.

Even death cannot stop me;

it is just a loss to the flesh

but an emancipation to my spirit.

So, to give up?

I haven't heard of that phrase.

It's not in my philosophy.

Not now and never will.

Samuel K. Anderson (Whispers from My Mother)

Whispers from My Mother

DAY 364

Ready or Just Lucky

You are not ready in life

if all you think about is luck.

Readiness is preparedness.

Preparedness is when all the pain of weakness

and excuses leave your mind, body and spirit through hard work.

Luck is the lazy folk's game of gamble.

So, come again;

are you ready or just lucky?

Samuel K. Anderson (Whispers from My Mother)

Whispers from My Mother

DAY 365

Climb It

You cannot depend
on people all the time.
It makes you weak eventually.
The mountain in front of you,
try to climb it alone.
Be adventurous.
Be complicated not easy to figure out.
Be daring.
Use grit to test your shortcomings
and work on them every day.

Samuel K. Anderson (Whispers from My Mother)

Whispers from My Mother

DAY 366

For the Leap Year

Never Forget

Never forget your journey.
One of the serious mistakes
in life is to forget how you
got to where you are.

Samuel K. Anderson (Whispers from My Mother)

Whispers from My Mother

Bonus & Final Words

They are Rare

There are some people in life
once you associate with them
your life turns out to be better
than it was before.
Be very good to such people.
They are rare.
They carry very unique
vibrations in the universe.

Samuel K. Anderson (Whispers from My Mother)

THE END

Whispers from My Mother

About the Author:

Samuel K. Anderson (MBA, BSBA, University of The Incarnate Word) is a Ghanaian Nigerian American citizen and a member of the largest leadership honor society in the nation (United States of America) known as NSLS, The National Society of Leadership and Success. He has served as an astute leader, motivator, philanthropist, father, entrepreneur, mentor, wisdom seeker and educator. He is a vibrant CEO and founder of two companies. A motivational and life coach speaker.

He has impeccable hands-on experience in banking, real estate, bankruptcy, life insurance, compliance, risk Samuel K. Anderson management, estate, probate, foreclosure, and investments. He served in his early formal education years as the Regional Trustee for the Eastern Regional Students' Representative Council with the Council's aim to Emancipate Students through Dialogue and a Philosophy of Non-Violence, President of an NGO that aimed at educating the youths on drug abuse, Counselor and Director of Children's Ministry. He completed formal bible training education/Seminary School and also studied Theology at Central University College before transitioning to San Antonio College then transferred to University of The Incarnate Word to pursue bachelor's degree in Accounting and an MBA with concentration in Asset Management (Real Estate and Finance).

www.ingramcontent.com/pod-product-compliance
Lightning Source LLC
Chambersburg PA
CBHW071215080526
44587CB00013BA/1382